ram lila-s
in
North India
and
Mauritius

Ram Lila-s
in
North India
and
Mauritius

Indrani Rampersad, Ph.D.

Former Senior Research Fellow in Ram Lila/Ramdilla Studies at The University of Trinidad and Tobago

Member of Research Committee, Ayodhya Research Institute, Ayodhya

VANI PRAKASHAN

VANI PRAKASHAN

4695, 21-A, Daryaganj, New Delhi 110 002
Phone : +91 11 23273167 **Fax :** +91 11 23275710
India
Branch
Ashok Rajpath, Patna 800 004
Coffee House Campus, Mahatma Gandhi Marg, Allahabad 211 001, (U.P)
Mahatma Gandhi International Hindi University, Vardha 442 001, Maharashtra
www.vaniprakashan.in
vaniprakashan@gmail.com
sales@vaniprakashan.in
In Association with

ESTD.-1986

Ayodhya Research Institute
presents

Ram Lila-s in North India and Mauritius
by Indrani Rampersad

ISBN : 978-93-87889-82-8
Religion/Culture

First Edition 2018

Price : 1495 / $ 30 / £ 15

Printed at M.S. Printers, Delhi-110 093 (India)

DEDICATION

For

Ramayan Premi-s

around the World

Research Facilitated by

The Academy for Arts, Letters, Culture and Public Affairs (The University of Trinidad and Tobago)

Grant from the Indian Council for Cultural Relations (ICCR), Government of India, The High Commission of India to Trinidad and Tobago

Mahatma Gandhi Institute for Cultural Cooperation, Trinidad and Tobago

Ayodhya Research Institute, autonomous organization of the Department of Culture, Government of Uttar

Photo Credits

Baxi-ka-Talab Ram Lila Committee, Rudhi Village

Bihar Pradeshik Marwari Sammelan

Petit Paquet Ramayan Mandali

Ayodhya Research Institute

Baxi-ka-Talab, Rudhi Village Ram Lila Committee

Bihar Pradeshik Marwari Sammelan

Vahini Geeta Ramsingh

Veenaud Boodhun

Other Photos by Dr. Pandita Indrani Rampersad

THE UNIVERSITY OF TRINIDAD AND TOBAGO

THE UNIVERSITY OF TRINIDAD AND TOBAGO
Administrative Office
O'Meara Campus
Lots #74-98 O'Meara Industrial Park, Arima
Telephone: (868) 642-8888 / 223-4888
Website: www.u.tt

Ref.**: UTT**.*Academy*.2018/012

2018 March 21st

Re**: Foreword -Pandita Indrani Rampersad PhD.: The Hidden Cultures: The Trinidad Ramlila**

Pandita's work, written in a clear, lucid style that demonstrates that she had foreigners in mind, explores the origins of the Ram Lilla-s are currently practiced, and the several common and different styles in use, including the Lila, the Dramatic-Theatrical, the Jhanki, as well as the Katha-Mimetic Movement, that can all be found in North India. Such styles enriched the Indian cultural traits and events carried out today in Fiji and the Caribbean, particularly those Ramlilla practices of Trinidad and Tobago. Her work shows too, the folk-theatre traditions of the Ram Lilla-s that are embellished by the rituals, bhakti, peripatetic movements, dance and mime, as the performers interpret the sacred narratives of Sree Ram and other deities concerned with the celebrations. Above all, the values of community bonding, as well as the importance of heritage and identity are all stressed within its pages, so that the reader will understand fully how important the celebrations were to the indentured Indians in the past and to those who today revere their Indian heritage and legacy.

Besides the pictures and drawings of stages and structures for the various theatres in the practice of the Ram Lilla-s, Pandita's work is accompanied by a multiplicity of photographs and tabled data that make for a more meaningful understanding of Indian traditions and the many geographical sites from which they originated and are practiced. Such data not only show the richness of the traditions but will help the readers to compare sites and stages in India and Trinidad, leading to a better understanding of how these traditions found their way to blossom on Trinidadian and other soils.

The pioneers of the University of Trinidad and Tobago therefore understood the importance of post graduate research, especially that of our hidden cultures; they sought to bring the work of the University to the yards of the ordinary folk of the community. Pandita's work, the Ram Lilla-s in North India will bring new light and a refreshing insight to the communities of the Caribbean and to scholars near and afar. Above all, it gives truth to the University's dream.

In education and culture,

Professor Hollis Liverpool
Professor of Calypso Art,
The Academy of Arts, Letters, Culture and Public Affairs

Ghansham Mohammed/Hollis Liverpool

MAURITIUS HIGH COMMISSIONER
NEW DELHI

Message from H.E. Mr. Jagdishwar Goburdhun, GOSK, High Commissioner of the Republic of Mauritius in India

This study is of paramount importance as such it is unique in itself as far as the research is concerned. The author has done tremendous effort in studying the celebration of Ramlila in Northern part of India and in Mauritius. It reminds of his historic speech made by Shri Modiji, the Prime Minister of India last October 2016 at Aishbagh maidan in Lucknow where he said that this is a land of buddh (knowledge) and not yudh (war). We must resolve to get freedom from these. Buddha's way or path should remain our ultimate destination, the Prime Minister says. He ends with a 'Jai Sri Ram' and the crowd was overwhelmed.

This book is well articulated and brushes a clear picture illustrated with catching photos in both countries where Ramlila is celebrated with pomp and éclat.

Ramlila, literally "Rama's play", is a performance of then Ramayana epic in a series of scenes that include song, narration, recital and dialogue. Traditionally organized in a makeshift open-air theatre at night, it is usually staged by amateur actors drawn from the same social grouping as the audience. It is performed across northern India during the festival of Dussehra, held each year according to the ritual calendar in autumn. Ramlila is a dramatic presentation of the whole life of Lord Rama, which starts from the history of Rama of his young age and ends up with the battle for 10 days between the Lord Ram and Ravan. According to the great Hindu epic Ramayana, Ram Lila is an old religious and cultural tradition that plays on stage every year for the 10 successive nights. A big fair is held during this period so that everyone may enjoy fair and Ram Lila drama. Ram Lila has more importance in the Indian culture. At most places in India, Ramlila held in Avadhi version of the Ramayana, Ramcharitmanas. Ramlila during dussehra attracts the global attention of the people. The Ramlila brings the whole population together, without distinction of caste, religion or age. All the villagers participate spontaneously, playing roles or taking part in a variety of related activities, such as mask- and costume making, and preparing make-up, effigies and lights.

Ramlila has received considerable global attention, especially due to its diverse representation throughout the globe, especially amongst the Indian Diaspora community, and regions where Hinduism has spread over the centuries, like Africa and several South East Asian countries. Unesco has proclaimed the tradition of Ramlila a Masterpiece of Oral and Intangible Heritage of Humanity in 2005.

Dr Indrani Rampersad has really done an empirical research and this type of studies should be encouraged otherwise in the very near future the coming generation will show no interest and the landscape of folklore will be washed away and to prevent this cultural erosion I humbly convey the message that more folklore studies should be incorporated in the prospectus of the university. Bravo to Dr Pampersad.

Jagdishwar Goburdhun, GOSK
High Commissioner

विश्वदीप दे
BISHWADIP DEY
उच्चायुक्त
HIGH COMMISSIONER

सत्यमेव जयते

भारतीय उच्चायोग
पोर्ट ऑफ स्पेन
त्रिनिडाड एवं टोबैगो
HIGH COMMISSION OF INDIA
P.O. BOX 530
PORT-OF-SPAIN, TRINIDAD & TOBAGO

PHONE: (868) 627-7485
FAX NO: (868) 627-6985
E-MAIL: hc.pospain@mea.gov.in
WEBSITE: www.hcipos.in

07 February 2017

Foreword

The essential unity underlying the rich diversity in Indian Culture is gleaned best from the numerous festivals and performances joyously celebrated throughout the year across the country and the diaspora. Ram Lila is the traditional performance of India's great epic poem, the Ramacharitmanas, and usually, runs for ten days during the period of Navratri (autumn in North India) and is most popular in North and Central India.

2. In response to the Government of India's nomination, the UNESCO has proclaimed Ram Lila as **Oral and Intangible Heritage of Humanity in 2005**, and inscribed Ram Lila on the **Representative List as a Heritage to be safeguarded** in 2008.

3. In the above context, I welcome Dr. Indrani Rampersad's brief survey of nineteen Ram Lilas in North India and in Mauritius as an important safeguarding initiative to preserve Ram Lila as an Oral and Intangible Heritage of Humanity.

4. Dr. Rampersad's research continues in Trinidad, Guyana, Suriname, Mauritius and Fiji covering the indentured North Indian diaspora. During 18th and 19th centuries, Indians migrated to these places under various compulsions. But they maintained the major epic of India – Ramcharitmanas – by recitation and drama thus etching the fervour in their minds and hearts. Thus, the folk tradition took shape which became a source of moral, spiritual and emotional support for the Indians, at their new home away from home.

5. I trust that the book will be useful not only for the Trinidadian or diaspora scholars, but to the general public also who may wish to read the book to appreciate the evolution of Ram Lila, and its continued relevance today. I congratulate Dr. Indrani Rampersad for presenting her research in the form of a book.

(Bishwadip Dey)

Foreword

Ravindra Nath Mahara (Ravi-ji)
Director, Bal Ramdilla,
Heritage Vacation Course,
The Hindu Prachar Kendra.

[Ravi-Ji is a certified and registered Cultural Worker and Mentor, in Traditional Knowledge and, Festival Development, with the National Registry of Artists and Cultural Workers, Ministry of Community Development, Culture and The Arts, Trinidad and Tobago]

Pandita Indrani has always been close to the Hindu community, either through her role as a Pandita, journalist, teacher or community worker. It is this drive that led her to study Asian Performance Theory: India under iconic performance guru, Richard Schechner at New York University in 2006. These studies exposed Pandita to Ramdilla as an academic subject. She became an advisor to the Heritage Vacation Course which has been experimenting with the Bal Ramdilla performance as a method for Heritage learning for children ages 5-19.

Pandita was granted the Senior Research Fellowship in Ram Lila/Ramdilla Studies at the new University of Trinidad and Tobago. Since then, she has pursued her research in Trinidad vigorously, then expanding her interest in the Caribbean region and its former British colonies. Eventually, she headed for India where she traveled extensively and even went as far as Mauritius and Fiji.

For Ramdilla practitioners from the Caribbean and the wider Gitmitya Mandal -Indenture diaspora - information was scarce because it was rarely shared. Academia focused more on indentureship, Ramayan, Hindi, and Bhojpuri, with little on the folk traditions andsimply nothing on the Ramdilla performance.

Hence, Pandita's remark, "I was surprised to learn that Mauritius did not have a vibrant open-air Ram Lila tradition." Academic studies on Ramdilla in the Caribbean is recent. It took a long time after this art-form was proclaimed by UNESCO as, "a Masterpiece of the Oral and Intangible Heritage of Humanity," for Ramdilla to enter the academic field in Trinidad and Tobago.

As an organizer of Bal Ramdilla and teacher of Ramdilla Arts and Management, I was deeply affected by the absence of the necessary information to build classes and organize the performance. By and large, an organizer turns to current practices and memories. There was little or no academic, artistic, or performative exchanges of best practices within the Girmitiyaa Mandal spread across the sugar plantations of the former British Empire. Pandita Indrani's scholarship has changed that.

She has facilitated access for the first time to four major areas of Ramdilla due to her travels, photographs, and accounts :

1) We have an opportunity to look at the costumes, face paintings, settings and colors of the performance;
2) We can view the arrangement of the performative space;
3) We have a view of both the similarities and differences in Ramdilla as a performative art practiced in the Caribbean, Mauritius and India;
4) It has deepened the relationship with peoples of the Girmitiya Mandal.

It is with gratitude therefore that Bal Ramdilla and the Heritage Vacation Course of Trinidad and Tobago welcomes this publication.

Table of Contents

Acknowledgements 17
Introduction 19
The West Indies/Caribbean 23
Mauritius 24
Ram Lila in North India 26
- Origins 26
- Performance Space of Ram Lila in North India 28
- Rangamandap/Rangashala/Pavilion Stage 28
- Elevated Platform Stage 29
- Traverse Stage 30
- Proscenium Stage. 31
- Thrust Stage 33

Rangavata Type of Stage also called open-air or khula maidan stage where the earth is the stage 35
Found Space 39
Mixed (combination of different performance spaces) 42
Ram Lila Performance Styles in North India 42
- Dramatic/Theatrical.
- LILA style
- Jhanki

Ram Lila Abhinaya (Movement and Gestures) 45
- (1) Angika Abhinaya
- (2) Vachik Abhinaya
- (3) Aharya Abhinaya
- (4) Sattvika Abhinaya

Aishbagh, Lucknow 46
Akbarpur, Ramabai Nagar, Kanpur Dehat 48
Anvarat Ram Lila at Tulsi Smarak Bhavan, Ayodhya Research Institute (ARI), Ayodhya 55
Baal Ramlila Committee, Japti, Wazirganj, Faizabad 59
Baxi-ka-Talab Dashara Mela (Ram Lila maidan, Badi Bazaar, Rudhi, Sitapur Road), Lucknow 62
Baxi-ka-Talab, Rudhi Village, Lucknow. 65
Bhagwatacharya Smarak Sadan, Sringharhat, Ayodhya 69
Bihar Pradeshik Marwari Sammelan, Bihar 71
Buxar, Bihar 72
Goswami Tulsidas Ram Lila Samiti, Sant Tulsipuri, Bhadaini, Varanasi 75
Jaswantnagar, Etawah 79

Masks at Jaswantnagar 87
More Masks 91
Weapons used by Ravan Sena/Army 93
Lanka/Rawan Minar in Kalpi: Where Rawan Does Not Die 94
Purabazar, Faizabad. 96
Rajendra Niwash, Swargdwar, Tulsinagar, Ayodhya 103
Ramnagar, Varanasi 106
Sahabganj, Ayodhya 109
Sri Ram Lila Samiti, Koonch, Jalaun, Bundelkhand 116
Shri Shishu Baal Ram Lila Samiti, Phool Wali Gali, Lucknow 120
Sri Public Bal Ram Lila Samiti, Lila Ground, Lohiyaa, Chowk, Lucknow 124
Indira Gandhi National Centre for the Arts (IGNCA) and Sangeet Natak Akadami 128
Ram Lila in Mauritius 129
Select Bibiography 134

Acknowledgements

- The Academy for Arts, Letters, Culture and Public affairs (The Academy) at the University of Trinidad and Tobago (UTT) for the fellowship on Ram Lila/ Ramdilla Studies from 2007 to 2012
- Professor Kenneth Ramchand (Associate Provost of The Academy for most of my fellowship)
- Professor Dr Hollis Liverpool, Professor of Carnival Arts and Program Professor at the Academy
- Ravi-Ji (Ravindra Nath Maharaj), former Govermor at UTT
- High Commissioner of India and Mahatma Gandhi Institut
- Shri MM Sharma, Director of the Mahatma Gandhi Institute for Cultural Cooperation (MGICC) in Trinidad and Tobago for the ICCR Grant to study Ram Lila in North India
- Dr. Yogendra Pratap Singh, Director of The Ayodhya Research Institute (ARI)
- Avinash Kumar (deceased) and Dharmendra Kr. Gupta of ARI
- Journalist Ashish Kumar Mishra of Bihar
- Mr. Veenaud Boodhun, Mrs Vidya Boodhun, Vicky and Vanysha Boodhun.
- Mr. Jugdishwur Goburdhun, President, Kissan House, Coudan, and current High Commissioner of Mauritius to India
- Mr. Ragoonath Deeal of Rashtriya Swayamsevak Sangha, Mauritius

Introduction

This publication is the outcome of original research started on Ram Lila in the Caribbean at the University of Trinidad and Tobago, from 2007. The research then expanded, with a research grant, to include North India in October 2010, At the kind invitation of Mr. Veenaud Boodhun and family, I was able to visit Mauritius from Oct. 28 to Nov. 6, 2010 to study Ram Lila there.

In October 2016, I visited Fiji to study their Ram Lila, This has all expanded and enriched the initial research into one that now covers Ram Lila in the indentured North Indian diaspora. This publication, however, gives a bird's eye view of Ram Lila in several parts of North India in October 2010 and a report on Ram Lila in Mauritius.

The LILA style of Ram Lila started in North India and made its way to the indentured or girmitiya diaspora in places like Trinidad (with over 20 LILA style performances), Guyana (where it went into extinction and was revived in 2007), Suriname (with three LILA style performances, today) and Fiji, where this researcher found only one performance resembling the LILA style - in Labasa - and this had moved from the open-air setting to its current setting in a large hall, covered, with open sides and retaining many elements of LILA style.

In 2010, in North India, Ram Lila was facing strong competition from the Devi Navratri Puja celebrations. It is crucial to document the various performance styles of telling the story of Ram and to evaluate the role and status of this performance in individual and community life.

Journalist Ashish Kumar Mishra of Bihar, was extremely helpful in helping me to locate the Ram Lila in Buxar. He lamented the decline in Ram Lila performances in Bihar. An interesting discovery in my research was the presence of two Ram Lila-s where Ravan does not die, viz. Jaswantnagar in Etawah and Kalpi in Kanpur.

The literature in English on Ram Lila in India tends to portray the Ramnagar Ram Lila at Varanasi, as the premier performance. Undoubtedly, the Ramnagar Ram Lila is special but there are many Ram Lila-s in rural communities across North India that remain largely unnoticed by researchers. Western scholars should be credited, however, with heightening awareness about and documenting Ram Lila.

Western academia affords many academic opportunities for Ram Lila reseach, while Indian academia is yet to offer its scholars similar incentives, leaving the field lacking in rich Emic perspectives.

Foremost among Ram Lila scholars is Richard Schechner (1989, 1977), who has written extensively on the Ram Lila in Ramnagar. Otherscholars include Norvein Hein (1958,1972); AnuradhaKapur (2006); Sarah Bonnemaison andChristine Macy (Bonnemaison and Macy 1990); Philip Lutgendorf (1991, 1992); Paula Richman (2010); Suresh Awasthi (1989); and William Sax (1990). Scholars who have written onRam Lila in Trinidad include RavindraNathMaharaj (2006), Indrani Rampersad (2011, 2018), PaulaRichman (2010), Milla C Riggio (2010), SatnarineBalkaransingh (2016) and Primnath Gooptar (2015).

There are many untold stories of Ram Lila performances in India that are organized, enacted and viewed by communities, generating a special community bonding and identity amongst them. While these may not have the patronage of big names and big money, they are really of the people, by the people and for the people. These performances exhibit the rich, traditional and popular heritage of North India and its diaspora. As recognized by UNESCO (2005), these kinds of performances are vulnerable and are central to the identity of communities and peoples.

The Marriage, Aishbagh, (2010).

Vaishnava Worship

Vaishnava devotional worship generally focuses on four aspects of the Lord viz. name or nām (fulfilled through jap), form or r p (fulfilled through ritual worship of the image through puja and seva), pilgrimage or dhâm (fulfilled by making yatras to sacred places associated with the avatar's life on earth) and l l (catching hold of the Lord's lila-s through recitation and katha; and seeing them enacted). L l is a "way of life" for devotees of Ram and Krishna. Vaishnava theologians recognize two types

(Lutgendorf 250)

Performing the Text

Three Genres of performing the text include "simple recitation, recitation plus exposition, and full dramatic enactment..."

1. Recitation - Private recitation (path) e.g. householders reciting the text over a period of time; public, time-bound recitation e.g. nine night Ramayan Yajna with recitation and exposition that is popular in the Caribbean
2. Kathakara–professional reciter-singer-artiste, sometimes called a Rama-Kathakara or a Hari-Kathakara.
3. Enactments of Ramcharitmanas - dramatic/theatrical and LILA.

(Lutgendorf 38, 39)

Ram Katha

Ram Katha refers to a traditional and ancient Indian storytelling style used by Lav and Kush (sons of the King Ram) to spread the story of their parents, Sita and Ram, accompanied by instruments, music and mime. " Katha" , in the context of Ramcharitmanas, refers to narration of the text that is "slow, systematic, storytelling recitation, interspersed with prose explanations, elaborations, and homely illustrations of spiritual points ... the role of the hearer (rot) is participatory rather than passive" (Lutgendorf 115). The definition holds true for the Caribbean also, where a "katha" incorporates religious ritual, bhakti, rasa, singing, music, and performance.

Katha Style

Katha style of reciting Ramcharitmanas includes :

- Religious rituals
- Bhakta-s (devotees) and shrota-s (listeners)
- Musical accompaniment
- Vyas tells the sacred story in rhythmic recitation style, making commentaries along the way
- Audience of devotees

Ram Lila in Tulsi Ghat, Varanasi, (2010).

Table I: Ram Lila Performances in North India and Mauritius

State	*City*	*Ram Lila Group*	*Nature of Performance Space*	*Style of Performance*	*Viewed*
UP	Lucknow	1. Aishbagh, Lucknow	Permanent roscenium manch in Ram Bhavan, Thrust Stage in open air	Dramatic, theatrical styleincluding mime, taped dialogue; sound and light effects, Vyas who recited in traditional style from the Manas	Yes
UP	Kanpur Dehat	2. Akbarpur, Ramabai Nagar, Kanpur Dehat	Open air, multiple locations, jhanki; few permanent structures like Talab	LILA style, including ime, jhanki, dialogue and a Vyas who recited in traditional style from the Manas	Yes
UP	Ayodhya	3. Anvarat Ram Lila at Tulsi Smarak Bhavan, Ayodhya Research Institute, Ayodhya	Manch inside an auditorium	Dramatic theatrical style with a vyas who recited in traditional style from the Manas	Yes
UP	Faizabad	4.BaalRam Lila Committee, Japti, Wazirganj, Faizabad.	Temporary manch in open air space with audience seated on the ground	Dramatic theatrical style with a vyas who recited in traditional style from the Manas	Yes
UP	Lucknow	5. Baxi-ka-Talab Dashara Mela ((Ram Lilamaidan, Badi Bazaar, Rudhi, Sitapur Road), Lucknow	Temporary manch under a tent that stood in open air. Audience sat on chairs under the tent	Dramatic theatrical style with sound and light effects, vyas who recited in traditional style from the Manas	Yes
UP	Lucknow	6. Baxi-ka-Talab, Rudhi Village, Lucknow	Permanent manch; open air stage; platform manch	Mixed LILA style and dramatic theatrical style that included miming and a vyas who recited in traditional style from the Manas	No
UP	Ayodhya	7.Bhagwatacharya Smarak Bhavan Ram Lila, Sringharhat, Ayodhya	Temporary proscenium manch constructed in open air with audience seated on ground	Dramatic, vyas	Yes
Bihar	Patna	8.Bihar Pradeshik Marwari Sammelan, Gandhi maidan, Patna.	Open-air, manch, Jhanki on Dussehra Day	Jhanki, dramatic theatrical, vyas	No
Bihar	Buxar	9.Buxar, Bihar	Temporary proscenium manch in open air and Jhanki	Dramatic theatrical, Jhanki, vyas who recited Ramcharitmanas	Yes
UP	Varanasi	10.Goswami Tulsidas Ram Lila Samiti, Sant Tulsipuri, Bhadaini, Varanasi	Open-air , mandir courtyard, mandir space, streets	LILA style, mimetic, Jhanki-s, Processions, vyas who recited Ramcharitmanas	Yes
UP	Etawah	11. Jaswantnagar, Etawah	Permanent manch in Ram Lila Building, open-air, multiple locations	Mixed LILA style and dramatic theatrical, miming, vyas who recited Ramcharitmanas	Yes
UP	Kalpi, Jalaun	12. Lanka/Rawan Minar : Where does not die. Kalpi Jalaun	Jalaun Permanent manch; open air.	Viewed performance space and spoke with residents	No
UP	Faizabad	13.Purabazaar Village, Faizabad	Permanent manch; open air.	LILA style, miming, dialogue, vyas who recited	Yes

UP	Ayodhya	14. Rajendra Niwash, Swargdwar, Tulsinagar, Ayodhya	Temporary proscenium manch in open-air	Ramcharitmanas Dramatic theatrical, vyas who recited Ramcharitmanas	Yes
UP	Varanasi	15. Ramnagar, Varanasi	Temporary manch in open air , traverse stage, end stage, Open-air, multiple Locations	Dramatic theatrical, miming, Jhanki, processional	Yes
UP	Ayodhya	16. Sahabganj, Ayodhya	Temporary manch in open air	LILA style, miming, dialogue, Vyas who recited verses of Ramcharitmanas	Yes
UP	Koonch, Jalaun	17. Shri Ram Lila Samiti, Konch, Jalaun.	Permanent manch, open-air, multiple locations	LILA style and miming, combined with dramatic theatrical style on the manch, dialogue, Vyas who recited from the Ramcharitmanas	Yes
UP	Lucknow	18. Shri Shishu Baal Ram Lila Samiti, Phool Wali Gali, Lucknow.	Permanent proscenium manch in a building	Dramatic, theatrical, vyas who recited Ramcharitmanas	Yes
UP	Lucknow	19. Sri Public Bal Ram Lila Samiti, Lila Ground, Lohiyaa, Chowk, Lucknow.	Temporary proscenium manchunder a tent in open-air	Dramatic theatrical, vyas who recited Ramcharitmanas	Yes

Open Air Demonstration of snippets of Ram Lila by IGNCA and Sangeet Natak Akadami

Delhi	Delhi	20. Indira Gandhi National Centre for the Arts (IGNCA) and Sangeet Natak Akadami	Open air Demonstration of events in Ram Lila	Stylized	Yes

Ram Lila in Mauritius

Mauritius	-	Mauritius	-	Dramatic theatrical and jhanki	No

Vyas prepares to read from the Ramacharitmanas at Ram Lila, Tulsi/Assi Ghat, Varanasi, (2010).

LILA STYLE OF PERFORMING RAM KATHA

The LILA style of performing the sacred narrative of Sree Ram (Ram Katha), as told in Ramcharitmanas, is marked by the lokadharmi style (realistic and amateur theatre conventions), religious ritual, bhakti, peripatetic movement, and miming conventions. It is a split, open-air performance that moves between two values (dharma and adharma) symbolized by Ayodhya and Lanka and between Vishnu Loka (the eternal abode of Lord Vishnu) and Mother Earth symbolizing the avatar. The LILA style is uniquely strong in satwik abhinaya and mime, and an avenue for darshan, community bonding, and healthy recreation (Pandita Indrani and Ravi-Ji, 2016).

UNESCO, on November 25, 2005, declared the traditional performance of Ram Lila as one of that year's 43 new Masterpieces of the Oral and Intangible Heritages of Humanity.

These awards are "an international distinction destined to raise public awareness of the value of this heritage, which includes popular and traditional oral forms of expression, music and dance, rituals and mythologies, knowledge and practices concerning the universe, know-how linked to traditional crafts, as well as cultural spaces. Often vulnerable, this heritage, a repository of cultural diversity, is essential to the identity of communities and peoples" (UNESCO 2005).

Ram Lila in North India

Origins

Many credit Megha Bhagat with starting the Ram Lila performance circa 1625 CE; others say it was Tulsi Das; and yet others point to the tradition of enacting Ram's story in dance-drama style that predated Tulsidas. Hein sees the birth of Ram Lila as emanating from "the ancient dance drama under the influence of forces like those which are altering the technique of the Yakshagânâ. We suppose that it took shape in North India between A.D. 1200 and 1500. It was one of the readjustments toward simpler art forms made necessary by the intrusion into Hindustan of an overwhelming Muslim culture" (Hein 105-125; Varadpande 263-264).

There are some legends about where the first Ram Lila in history started and Assi/Tulsi Ghat is one place so mentioned.

According to one legend, Tulsidas' disciple, Megha Bhagat, started the first Ram Lila at Nati Imli in Benares after Tulsidas' passing and after having a dream to dramatize the Bharat Milap at Nati Imli. During the Milap, Bhagat reportedly died in ecstasy. It was around 1625, that this Ram Lila is said to have come into vogue. The Maharaja of Benares always visits this performance, missing the day's performance at his own Ramnagar Ram Lila ("Bharat Milap at Nati Imli Finds Rapt Attention").

Dr. Induja Awasthi ("History of Indian Theatre" 303) avers that Tulsidas started the first Ram Lila, inspired, one day, from reciting the Valmiki Ramayana on his way to his Assi home. He first presented the Jhanki of Rama's coronation, leading to the "Assi ki Rama Leela" which is still conducted by the Goswami Tulsidas Ka Akhada at what is now Tulsi Ghat (Assi Ghat once included the area now called Tulsi Ghat). Tulsidas was the first Head or Mahanta of this Akhada.

In an interview with Bhanu Shankar Mehta (2009 - 2015), he described four manch-s in Ram Lila: (i) at the north, is Ayodhya/Raja manch with seven steps, where the swaroopa-s sit; (ii) at the south, there are five steps where the kings sit; (iii) women sit in the east; (iv) and in the west are the Ramayani-s and the audience. Mehta said Tulsidas used the Lila to deliver Dharma teachings in an artistic way to people who were mainly illiterate; Tulsidas had studied drama, puppet theatre, etc., so he knew about dramatic techniques. Mehta believed that were female performers in ancient times, but this changed with Bharat (Mehta 2009).

Hein believed that there were Sanskrit nataka-s (dramas) on Ramayana themes before the sixteenth century, but their objective was not "to make a sacred writing understood and appreciated" as in the Ram Lila and they did "not possess enough of the R ml l 's characteristics to have been its progenitor." He did date the Ram Lila before the sixteenth century. Tulsidas knew of the LILA style of storytelling because, in Ramcharitmanas, Kak Bhushundi mentioned it as one of his childhood activities in a previous birth (Hein, 18, 110 - 111).

Ram Lila space and performance style show both Sanskrit and Prakrit influences. In the late 1800s in India, a new kind of drama emerged due to westernization but it did not drastically change the Indian stage and plays because of the vibrant performing arts traditions in many places. The folk theatre in Tamil Nadu, for example, was hugely popular even with its influential group of English educated people. While innovations were taking place within the tradition, there was "no radical departure from it." People were experimenting with modern drama within traditional frameworks (Das 273). Those experimentations led to the predominance of the manch stage in most of the Ram Lila-s of UP and Bihar – stages that were enclosed on three sides.

Theatre structures existed in ancient India before the time of Bharata of Natya Shastra (NS) and theatre architecture reached perfection in the age of Bharat says Iravati. Aside from the open-air theatre, therse were the cave theatres that were permanent structures located on hilltops, where the tranquillity was conducive to theatrical shows associated with yajna-s and related festivities, and where performers were not likely to be disturbed. Iravati avers that caves were used as theatres in ancient India and for small and private audiences, based on size and literary references (187-195).

Mehta argued that the basic design (bare stage with four poles and roof) of the early pavilion stage in early Indian theatre continues today. He referred, not to open air stages, but to theatres in an auditorium type of setting. The advances in architectural design and construction over time and the new needs of elite patrons would have influenced the design of the playhouse, said Mehta. The design, size, shape, and ornamentations could vary depending on the needs of society's elite. The stage faced East and was slightly elevated, with space for musicians (Mehta 39-41).

The dressing room was located backstage where properties and costumes were stored. A partition with two doors connected the backstage with the main stage, said Mehta. The floor of the auditorium was polished and this is where the viewers sat. A prominent seat was reserved in the front row for the chief patron. There were also raised platforms and galleries with different enclosures for different spectators (Mehta 40-45).

The size of the playhouse varied. It could be square, rectangular, oblong, circular, or triangular. The pillars were ornamental and ceilings painted. The walls were covered with fresco paintings. There were many altars and high windows. "The playhouses were built round the focal point of the stage proper and the seat of the chief patron." The theatres were small and intimate and catered to a select audience, which was close and near to the performance area (Mehta 40-45).

Music Band at the Ram Lila with policemen for crowd control at Jaswant Nagar, (2010).

Performance Space of Ram Lila in North India

Ram Lila is performed in a variety of community spaces, mainly "found space" in India. Both the LILA style and the dramatic/theatrical style were found in open air spaces in the North Indian Ram Lila held during the Navratri period in 2010. Sometimes the LILA style was combined with the dramatic/theatrical style, with part of the performance held in open-air spaces and part on small proscenium stages, either ensconced in nearby buildings or on temporarily constructed stag es in the open-air with audiences seated on the ground.

The Ram Lila that was recouped in the Caribbean from the memories of the indentured Indians took place in "found spaces" on sugar estates and community grounds and was in LILA style.

Suriname had experimented with moving from the LILA style to the dramatic/theatrical style inside a theatre auditorium but it was not successful and they returned to the open-air community space and LILA style. In recent years, some groups in Trinidad and Guyana have also taken Ram Lila to the manch, inside of or next to a mandir. However, the majority of Lila-s are still performed in community space by community groups using the earth as performance space. No doubt there is need for dramatic/theatrical, natya elements catering to an elite audience but it should replace the LILA style of performance which is community based.

In India, Ram Lila takes place in different kinds of performance spaces. There is the manch stage and its variants; mandap/pavilion stage; thrust stage; maidan (open-air, community space where the earth is the stage); multiple locations (different events are performed in different geographical areas); found space (e.g. street); and mixed space (combination of various performance space types).

Stage Types

Rangamandap/Rangashala/Pavilion Stage

This type of mandap stage looks like a pavilion, shed, or open hall "with four pillars supporting a roof which was open on all sides or at least three sides;" it was temporary and sometimes permanent and built according to strict rules of Vastu Shastra (Mehta 37-40). The mandap stage seems to have been the most popular type of stage in ancient India, became the prototype for theater structures in India, and is today popular in Ram Lila performances in North India. Thirteen of the nineteen that this researcher surveyed used some variant of the mandap.

According to Iravati, the early mandap style structures were temporary ones that eventually morphed into permanent ones. He recounted the sacred narrative of Lord Indra instructing the devata-s to construct a pavilion where the apsara-s would dance at the time of the Yajna performed by King Maurtta. Lord Indra had advised that a temporary pavilion be built with pillars and stairs leading to a raised stage. The spectators would sit around this pavilion to see the performance (Iravati 197). These temporary pavilions were highly decorated and eventually, they evolved into preksagriha-s or theatres where spectators sat inside the mandap to see the performances. Bharata mentions three shapes and sizes of theatres—oblong, square and triangular; and large, medium and small (Varadpande 247).

At Baxi-ka-Talab, Rudhi Village, there is a temporary mandap type of stage in the middle of the open-air performance area for part of the performance. The photo below shows Brahmins performing yajna under a mandap stage that has a thatched roof and four bamboo poles at the four corners supporting the roof. The raskshasa-s are seen on the outside disturbing the yajna.

Open-air performance space at Baxi-ka-Talab, Rudhi Village.

Above is another style of the earthen stage that is slightly raised and technically may be called a manch as it has a back wall, a roof and is open on three sides. It stands opposite the Sarveshwara Mahdeva Mandir which acts as a green room, where performers dress and perform Arti before starting the Ram Lila. This stage is slightly raised on two rows of building blocks and lepayed with a mixture of earth and cow dung. Four wooden temporary wooden poles support the canopy; the back of the stage is part of the adjoining permanent building, making this stage open on three sides. This stage becomes Ayodhyapuri during the Ram Lila.

Elevated Platform Stage

Below is another type of manch. It is a permanent, concrete, elevated platform stage with several steps. Today, it represents the Dandaka Forest. Ram and Lakshman sit at the highest level with other performers sitting on the lower steps. This is found at the Ram Lila in Purabazaar Village, Faizabad.

The photo above shows a similar elevated platform stage with concrete steps in the open-air at Akbarpur. This manch represents Chitrakoot. Here, Ram, Sita, and Lakshman

Row of concrete steps represent the mountain at Faizabad, (2010).

Raised step-like stage in the open-air at Lanka maidan in Akbarpur.

sit at the top with the Vyas and others are seated below as they await Bharat and Shatruhan who are coming across the Ganga.

Below left, at Sahabganj, is a mandap with an elevated stage made of benches to resemble a throne. This stage resembles those seen at Akbarpur and Purabazaar.

Traverse Stage

The traverse stage at Ramnagar is a long plank of wood raised above the audience seated on the earth. It is connected on either end by small end stages. Below is the end stage at one end of the traverse stage.

The swaroopa-s walk through the audience on the raised traverse stage to perform part of the Lila at this end. This traverse stage allows for greater intimacy between the audience and the swaroopa-s.

Throne like manch under a mandap at Sahabganj.

Open end of the traverse stage, Ramnagar, Varanasi, (2010).

Male dressed as a female singer in red sari sings traditional folk songs as the drummer plays dholak at one end of the stage. Ravan is seated on his throne (Shri Shishu Baal Ramlila Samiti, (2010).

Proscenium Stage

Below is a concrete proscenium stage, whose concrete flat roof is supported by six pillars, with the sides open. This is a variant of the rangamandap design and is found at Purabazaar, Faizabad.

Proscenium stage, Puraabazaar, Faizabad, (2010).

Proscenium stage in a hall at Shri Shishu Baal Ram Lila Samiti, Phool Walli Galli, Lucknow, (2010).

Above is a permanent manch (like a western proscenium stage) at Shri Shishu Baal Ramlila Samiti, Phool Wali Galli, Lucknow. This stage faces an open hall where the audience sits. The Lila is performed both on this manch and in the open-air area in front of it.

The photo shows performers reciting from the Ramcharitmanas before the Lila begins. The singers and musicians occupy space on the apron at down stage and stage

Temporary proscenium stage in open-air, Jaswantnagar, (2010).

right. The audience sits on the floor looking up at the action on the proscenium stage.

The photo at below left shows a temporary mandap at the southern end of the open-air maidan in Jaswantnagar where the Lila takes place. It is covered with cotton cloth at the back and its three sides are partially open. Its roof is a cotton canopy supported by four poles.

Ram and Sita greet their Guru on the manch at Thakurbari Hall.
Photo courtesy Bihar Pradeshik Marwari Sammelan

Below in Patna, the performers conduct the Lila for nine nights on a manch inside the Thakurbari Hall in Kadamkuan, Patna. Steps lead up to the stage performance area.

Thrust Stage

The Thrust stage is oblong, extending into audience space, allowing the audience to see the action from three sides. The upstage end of the Thrust stage connects to the backstage that functions as a proscenium stage at Aishbagh and Baxi-ka-Talab Dashara Mela (Lucknow). The Thrust stage allows for greater interaction and familiarity between performers and the audience.

Thrust stage joins the proscenium stage behind, at Aishbagh, (2010).

In the photo above, before the Lila begins, organizers reward members of their organization and the community for their dedication to Ram Lila. When the Lila takes place in the proscenium/ backstage area, photographers freely occupy the Thrust stage to get a better view.

Below is the Thrust stage at Baxi-ka-Talab Dashara Mela, Lucknow. This stage is attached to a traditional proscenium stage at the back. The performers use both spaces for the performance.

Thrust stage at Baxi-ka-Talab Mahotsav, Military Ground, Lucknow, (2010).

Stage inside a wall at Jaswantnagar, (2010).

Rangavata Type of Stage also called open-air or khula maidan stage where the earth is the stage

This type of performance space defines the LILA style of village India and which the indentured Indians took with them to the indentured diaspora during nineteenth century indentureship. The open-air performance spaces at Jaswantnagar and Faizabad resemble the traditional open- air spaces in places like Trinidad and Suriname.

Of the nineteen Ram Lila-s surveyed, the rangavata stage was noted at the following ten places :

1. Akbarpur (Kanpur Dehat)
2. Baxi-ka-Talab (Rudhi Village, Lucknow)
3. Bihar Pradeshik Marwari Sammelan (Patna, Bihar)
4. Goswami Tulsidas Ram Lila Samiti (Varanasi)
5. Jaswantnagar (Etawah)
6. Lanka/Rawan Minar (Kalpi, Jalaun)
7. Purabazaar Village (Faizabad)
8. Ramnagar (Varanasi)
9. Sahabganj (Ayodhya)
10. Shri Ram Lila Samiti, Koonch (Jalaun)

Rangavata stage was a cleared area of land space that was encircled by a railing made of thorns and pieces of wood used for archery contest among the Pandava princes (see Mehta 38). The spectators surrounded the performance on all sides. The reference to the thorns reinforces the origin of a barrier between performer and the public to prevent the public from entering the performance space.

Seventy-three-year-old, world-renowned Kathak dancer, musician, and choreographer, Birju Maharaj*, explained that in the open-air or khula maidan, since there is no wing or pardah (curtain) the performers perform on the ground and within a fence. He recalled, as a child, seeing Ram Lila in Faizabad and and Ayodhya where his uncle performed. In those days they performed on the ground, but slowly the performers moved from the ground to a manch. Performers were at that time also moving to the cinema hall where they used the stage for dance.

Dancing or performing on the earth with its unevenness etc. was difficult as opposed to dancing on the manch, which was much easier. In the former (performing on the earth), however, the audience was all around and closer to the performers than in the latter (Maharaj).

Kathak Master, Birju Maharaj

Mehta traces open-air performances to the Rig Veda where space was allocated for performers and the audience, and there was no physical demarcation between per former and audience. These open- air performance spaces were "the sites of sacrificial grounds, on top of a hill, a bank of a river, in parts of tree groves or even in pleasure gardens ...." with spectators watching the performance from all sides or sometimes three open sides. There was maximum interaction between performer and spectator making it very participative. "It was only when this atmosphere of rapport was disturbed that a need was felt to have some kind of an enclosure or a shelter," says Mehta (37).

In India, it is common to hear any performance of Ramayana or Ramcharitmanas described as Ram Lila regardless of it being a professional dramatic/ theatrical presentation on a stage or a LILA style presentation in the open-air by amateurs in a community.

Hein (70-71) addressed the issue when he noted that the term Ram Lila was used in North India to refer to dramas based on the subject matter and the Ramcharitmanas. "They cover the main incidents narrated in the R mcaritm nas in a series of performances lasting many days, and they employ a rare stage technique that combines recitation of the sacred text with simultaneous acting and dialogue." He also noted that the term "Ram Lila" sometimes referred to plays "produced at casual times by traveling companies of professional actors."

Hein (70-71) defined the great Ram Lila of North India as "a distinct social institution" associated with the annual dussehra holidays in late September. This was different from traditional forms of drama that he saw in Mathura District because it was "produced both by and for local people." He pointed to elected committees organising these dussehra Ram Lila-s. "This is the R ml l which touches the experience of the average person who grows up in North India." Hein was describing the oral traditions between

* Pandit Birju Maharaj was born in Lucknow on February 4, 1938, into a family of Kathak dancers with his father and uncles being experts . He was tutored in seeing the world as an artiste. He

1949-50. Yet, the same issue of the definition of "Ram Lila" remains unresolved today as India continues to use it as a depictive term for all dramatizations of Ramcharitmanas at any time of the year and in any style.

At Jaswantnagar, in the background (right), there is a small opening in a building that acts as a proscenium stage for small enactments, but the open ground in the middle is where action like yuddh-s or battles take place. This open ground is a street that was converted into an open-air maidani stage.

The photos below show part of the Jaswantnagar town square converted into performance space. Here is a circle within which two white heavy-duty plastic chairs are placed. Sita and Lakshman sit on these chairs as the two vyas' narrate the events leading up to Sita's kidnapping. The protective space made by Lakshman's Rekha encircles the performers shown in the photo.

The Lakshman Rekha is a protective circle dug into the earth with a stick and filled with potash, which will be set alight when Ravan tries to cross the Lakshman Rekha to kidnap Sita.

Inside the Protective circle or Lakshman Rekha, Jaswantnagar, (2010).

In Patna, the Bihar Pradeshik Marwari Sammelan hosts Ram Lila on both a manch and in the open-air.

The photo at below shows Lanka on fire with Hanuman leading his army at Gandhi Maidan.

Ordinary members of the public can be seen mingling with the army with Lanka on fire behind. Here the performance takes place in the open air with the earth as performance space. The ground looks unprepared.

Photos courtesy Bihar Pradeshik Marwari Sammelan, Patna.

Found Space

At Sahabganj, the Lila is performed in a narrow galli or lane that is blocked off for that purpose. A rope fence demarcates the performance space from audience space. In the background is the Ayodhya manch under a mandap structure. The action, however, took place on the street for the fighting parts of the Lila.

Ram and Lakshman seated on a rath (cart) pulled by a horse at Gandhi Maidan.
Photo courtesy Bihar Pradeshik Marwari Sammelan

At Akbarpur, the organizers have demarcated five performance spaces in different parts of the town but today they are using only three of them. This small performance space adjoins the Kalarang Talab or Lake that becomes Ganga for the crossing to the opposite side where Bharat Milap takes place in the Lanka maidan. The space is also under an ancient banyan tree - a tree that is sacred to Hindus.

Narrowgalli where Ram Lila is performed in Sahabganj, (2010).

A cotton sheet was spread on the earthen ground and the vyas and musicians sat on it, singing from the Ramcharitmanas. Others performed arti over the swaroopa-s. The divinities here were called "Bhagavan" and as they moved in procession* their pathway was strewn with flower petals. Audience members, young and old, touched their feet in reverence, though there was no rush for such darshan. After their rituals under the banyan tree, the performers then crossed over the Kalarang Talab (lake) in a boat. Before coming to this performance space, the performers got into costume, performed arti at the Sarveshwara Mahadeva Mandir, then took out their jhanki through the street.

Advocate Ayodhya Prasad Gupt Kumud.
Photo by Pandita Indrani, (2010).

Different lila-s (events) in the Ram Lila might be held in different geographical areas, e.g. Konch, Etawah.

The Konch Ram Lila in Etawah is well known for moving from place to place for different parts of the Lila. A similar style takes place in Akbarpur (Kanpur Dehat).

According to Advocate Ayodhya Prasad Gupt Kumud ("Sanskritik"), Ram Lila started there in 1851 and was performed in fourteen gardens on the borders of Konch. In 1910, the performance moved from these gardens to the manch in the town square (Kumud 2010). Konch is

**Processional entries is a dramatic style in Ram Lila at Konch . There are conventional rules for entering, gait, etc. See Mehta (215-216) for more.*

verdant with lots of gardens, woods and mandir-s on the outskirts of the town. Writing in 1858, Behan noted that, "Koonch is an open town; but it is difficult to attack because it is surrounded by woods, gardens and temples, with high walls round them, every one of which is a defence." The First War of Independence (1857-58) disrupted Ram Lila in its natural environment forcing it into the town square. Today some events (lila-s) in the Ram Lila take place in the town square while others take place in the Gardens on the outskirts. Advocate Gupta explained that during the day, part of the Lila takes place in the natural gardens of the area and during the evening, parts move to the manch in the town square. This was done for security reasons (the area was threatened by Naxalite violence). When the Lila takes place inside the town square, the audience sits on the ground looking up at the Lila on the manch that is permanent. Other locations are in "found" open air space in the town. In the Caribbean, there is only one Ram Lila that resembles this style-at Orange Valley, Vishnu Mandir, SDMS Branch # 150, Couva, Trinidad-where they move from the mandir (where a dramatic/theatrical enactment is done of Ram going into banwas or exile) to different points along the main street (where different lila-s are performed) culminating in the burning of a Ravan effigy in an open-air , savanna space.

The Jhanki of Ram and Lakshman arrives at found space under a banyan tree next to the Kalarang Talab (lake) in Akbarpur, (2010).

Open Air Performance Space at Baxi-ka-Talab.

Mixed (combination of different performance spaces)

This style is found especially in open-air spaces where the Lila is performed on the ground and organizers tend to stage parts of the Lila in the open air (with earth as the stage) and parts on a manch, e.g. at Baxi-ka-Talab, Rudhi Village (Lucknow), Purabazaar Village (Faizabad) and Jaswantnagar.

At Baxi-ka-Talab, Rudhi Village, in Lucknow, the organizers use a concrete proscenium stage for some parts of the action and the open air space and ground) for other action like the yuddh-s (wars and fights).

At Konch (Etawah), the Lila took place in different geographical areas using three different kinds of performance spaces-open air space in the town square with the earth as performance space, the gardens on the outskirts of the town, and the manch in the town square.

Ram Lila Performance Styles in North India

There are three main styles of performing Ram Lila : Dramatic/Theatrical; LILA; and Jhanki

Dramatic/Theatrical : This performance style occurred alone or in conjunction with other styles in at least fourteen (14) of the nineteen (19) performances that this researcher observed. It is evident in mandali-s or groups of professionals/semi-professionals who are roving performers. Conventions of modern theatre and ancient Sanskrit theatre influence this style. Traditional Indian aesthetics is evident in the aharya and presence of a vidusha (who provides entertainment), for example. This was evident in places like Buxar; Bhagwatacharya Smarak Bhavan (Ayodhya); Baxi-ka-Talab Dashara Mela (Ram LilaMaidan, Baidi Bazaar, Rudhi, Sitapur Road, Lucknow); Sri Public Ram Lila Samiti (Lila Ground, Lohiyaa Chowk, Lucknow); and Shri Shishu Baal Ram Lila Samiti, (Phool Wali Galli, Lucknow).

LILA style refers to an open-air, amateur, community-based enactment of Ramcharitmanas, narrated by a pandit/vyas in katha style, accompanied by religious songs and musical instruments, and using mime, movement and gestures to communicate meaning to an audience primarily of devotees. It also incorporates the jhanki style. The LILAstyle originated in rural North India and is found in villages like Faizabad (India), for example, and in the indentured North Indian diaspora like Trinidad, Suriname, and Fiji.

Today, it embraces dramatic/theatrical elements, as well.

Kapur notes that before dialogue was added to the Ramnagar Ram Lila, that the performers "remained silent while the Ramacharitmanasa was chanted" (1990:6). This underscores the paramount importance of listening (Sravanam) to the text while miming the story. Hein referred to researchers who described the Ram Lila's actors as being "voiceless", where the 'performance consists entirely of pantomimes, and to which the text is read out from the Râmâyaòa' [Niehus in Hein (1972, 77)], while Prinsep described the acting as a "dumb show." Hein saw the pantomime as secondary to the original style of Ram Lila predating the dialogue that was introduced by the modern Hindi plays (Hein, 1972, 77, 78). To Hein, the classical nataka or drama was the progenitor of Ram Lila (Hein, 1972, 111, 112). He saw a possible historical link between Ram Lila and the dance drama, attributing strong Moghul pressures to the "abandonment of the dance-drama's method for that of theRâmlîlâ." He concluded that Ram Lila "took shape in North India between C.E. 1200 and 1500 (1972, 124, 125).

The indentured Indians brought the LILA style from the villages of Uttar Pradesh and Bihar to the Caribbean and other parts of the indentured diaspora like Fiji. Here, the vyas/pandit narrates from the Ramcharitmanas, providing cues for the performance. As descendants of indentured Indians in places like Trinidad, lost their ancestral languages and could no longer comprehend the original text of Ramcharitmanas, the creative vyas/pandit began to translate the doha-s and chaupaiee-s and bhashyacommentaries into Trinidad English dialect. The microphone made its appearance in these open-air performances in the 1960s when organizers and narrators used it, mainly. Now, as dialogue replaces miming and with the advent of the cordless microphone, main performers are using use it increasingly.

Jhanki at VI International Ramayana Conference, Mauritius, August, (1990). *Photo courtesy Petit Paquet Ramayan Mandali*

Jhanki : A Jhanki literally means a glimpse – a glimpse of the deity. Jhanki-s in Ram Lila give a glimpse of some iconic event in the narrative. It "does not enact any narrative" and in it drama and image worship meet. The traditional Hindu worship which consists in the contemplation of the form of the deity is continued in jh ñk and is vivified by a divine response that direct, personal, and immediate (Hein, 1972, 17, 18).

In the Akbarpur jhanki, the swaroopa-s sat on a palanquin that was carried on the shoulders of men through the streets. Jhanki-s are also carried on vehicles that are ornately decorated. Organizers decide when they take out Jhanki-s e.g. the Bihar Pradeshik Marwari Sammelan in Patna takes out Jhanki-s on Dussehra day.

In Mauritius, jhanki sseem to have been popular in earlier times. Above is a jhanki of Ram, Sita and Lakshman by Petit Paquet Ramayan Mandali at VI International Ramayana Conference, Mauritius, August 1990.

Ram Lila Abhinaya (four-fold aesthetic means to experience rasa)

Abhinaya refers to all the aesthetic means that performers choose and design to draw the audience into their (performers') world and to ignite the desired emotions and meaning that they (performers) are seeking to communicate. In a traditional Indian performance, the performer desires to transport the audience to the mental and emotional state required for experiencing the rasa intended by the performer.

Ram Lila is a bhakta-oriented performance (where darshan is the goal). The message is spiritual, and the goal is to bring about spiritual transportation and transformation, and to teach and entertain. The highest goal for the audience is to experience darshan.

The Natya Shastra (NS) categorizes Abhinaya as four-fold: Angika (physical movement of body), Vachik (words and music), Aharya (dress, costume, make-up, setting etc.) and Saatwik (emotions).

(1) Angika Abhinaya refers to the physical ways that the performer moves the major and minor body limbs to communicate the rasa or emotion that s/he seeks to evoke in the darshaka. In the LILA style this was natural and realistic as against the stylized movements of the dramatic/theatrical style.

(2) Vachik Abhinaya refers, for example, to literary tools used in language and the kinds of sounds used in the performance with the intention of evoking intended rasa-s. Words and sound communicate ideas that the performer interprets through various abhinaya. Music helps to create a mood. In the Trinidad Ram Lila, the vyas recites the verses of the Ramcharitmanas to the accompaniment of percussion instruments and intersperses his recitation with an English translation of those verses. In translating, the vyas has to use story-telling skills of voice modulation and so on to communicate the message, to excite the audience and to direct the performers who are miming the meaning of what they are hearing. In Vachik Abhinaya in the Trinidad Ram Lila, tassa, jhal (brass cymbals) and tal play a central role in evoking rasa in fighting scenes, in particular. In North India in open-air Ram Lila-s like Akbarpur, Sahabganj and Jaswantnagar, brass bands and drums were used for similar effect.

(3) Aharya Abhinaya refers to the external decorations on the performer's body and the physical setting. It includes makeup and costuming, ornaments, use of specific colours, hairstyles, dress code for particular characters, open-air setting, stage props, décor and so on. In the LILA style, thE aharya abhinaya was simple though effective.

(4) Sattvika Abhinaya refers to the artistic creation of various emotions in the performer's mind. The combination of a great performer and a connoisseur darshaka will lead the latter to experience the emotions depicted by the performer. For example, a great performer, through fanning, perspiration, swooning, and so on, can move a darshaka to experience a grief similar to what s/he (the performer) is trying to communicate. In traditional Ram Lila, the sattvika emotions are the higher objectives.

In all the Ram Lila performances surveyed in North India, organizers paid special attention to aharya. This is true especially of the manch (stage) performances with their professional or semi-professional performers. There, the stage setting, costumes, jewellery, make-up, and hairstyles are all professionally done and elaborate. In performances that combined open-air and manch, the same elaborate attention to aharya was noticed. In all the performances, the special characters (swaroopa-s and kings, for example) were elaborately dressed. In performances that received heavy funding (e.g. Baxi-ka-Talab DasharaMela, Ram Lila Maidan, Baidi Bazaar, Rudhi, Sitapur Road, Lucknow), the aharya was far more elaborate than those that were not so fortunate, especially if they relied on committees and collections from the community (e.g. Baxi-ka-Talab, Rudhi Village).

Aishbagh, Lucknow

On October 9, 2010, the Ram Lila at Aishbagh, Lucknow performed the Dhanush Yajna. This Lila used to be performed in the open air up to 2006, when it moved to the manch and its present format, according to organizers, Harish Chandra Agrawal and Aditya Devedi. This year, light and sound,

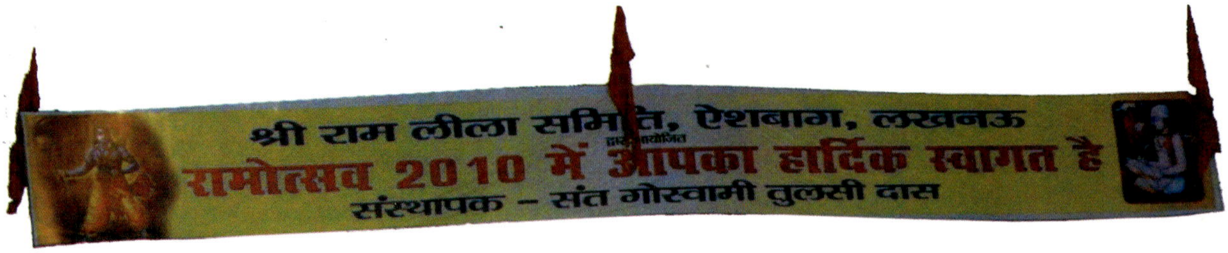

computer technology and the big projector screen are the highlights. The big projector screen showed pre-recorded scenes of Hanuman flying across the ocean, Lakshman Rekha on fire, and arrows flying between Ram and Rawan (Jain, 2010).This kind of innovation is an added attraction to the professional manch presentation.

Interestingly, the Ram Lila is preceded by an enactment of the birth of another Vishnu avatar, Krishna. This is a tradition in several Ram Lila performances in North India and some perform it either before or after the Ram Lila. In 2010,

In the photo at left, Ram lifts the Bow as pre-recorded light and sound effects (lighting and thunder) provide dramatic effect. Thunder roars and lightning flashes in the skies as Sri Ram breaks the Bow.

Agra saw the revival of Krishna Lila at the Balkeshwarmaidan. Krishna Lila seems to have declined as Ram Lila ascended in popularity, in the past. It's the same experience in Trinidad where Krishna Lila gave way to Ram Lila. In India, today's Krishna Lila is being patterned on a style similar to Ram Lila and performed for ten days (Khandelwal). Many claim that Ram Lila was patterned on the Krishna Lila which predated it.

The special characters like the swaroopa-s, kings, and queens wear special dress, colors, make-up, crowns, hairstyles, etc. as seen below.

The Lila was performed on a proscenium stage attached to a thrust stage on the ground floor of the huge

Krishna Lila at Aishbagh, Lucknow, before the Ram Lila begins.

L to R : Lakshman, Ram, Sita and Dasharatha at Aishbagh Ram Lila, (2010).

Organizers at Aishbagh Ram Lila : Aditya Devedi and Harish Chandra Agrawal (L to R), (2010).

Ram Bhavan (see photo below). The audience sits on chairs facing the stage.

At Aishbagh Ram Lila dialogue delivery is in professional style. Here there are no unsightly microphones. Instead, the dialogue is pre-recorded and the performers mime as the recording is played. This is the only Lila where the researcher saw this technique being used. This allowed for the use of sound effects along with the speech. The speech was not in the oratorical declamatory style of Ramnagar and Varanasi, but done in theatrical/dramatic style.

Here the vyas was seated on a separate and higher stage called Tulsi manch from where he recited appropriate Ramcharitmanas verses to the accompaniment of musical instruments. The fact that this manch was named after Tulsidas, reinforces the fact that the vyas is the voice of Tulsidas in the Lila.

The multi-media approach to Ram Lila at Aishbagh makes the big screen a new dimension of the performance area. The big screen is not just used to broadcast the performance and specially recorded events. At the Ram Lila of the Baxi-ka-Talab Dashara Mela (Lucknow), the side screens cater to audience members who might be sitting out of the direct line of vision of the stage performance.

Akbarpur, Ramabai Nagar, Kanpur Dehat

At Akbarpur in Kanpur Dehat, the performance was very different from all the other Ram Lila performances that this researcher saw. Anand Gupta explained that the Sarveshwara Mahadeva Mandir was built in 1895 and the Lila starts from there. This Lila, the organizers said, is registered with the Uttar Pradesh Government (Registration number 496/1860). This registration allows them to get grants from Government for cultural activities like the Ram Lila performance.

There were four performance spaces where the Lila took place. The first space was Ayodhyapuri, which is in front of the Sarveshwara Mahadeva Mandir and is just an open stage. The stage is very

Performers at Aishbagh Ram Lila, 2010.

Above shows some of the performers at Aishbagh. Their costume resembles those in most other places and they seem to be mass-produced.

simple and blends in with the surrounding environment. The Lila begins every day from this Mandir where the performers don their dress and make-up and perform arti. The other performance spaces are Janakpuri, Kalarang Talab, and Lankapuri maidan.

On this day of the Lila (October 12, 2010), Bharat and Shatrughana travel across the Ganga (Kalarang Talab) to Chitrakoot (in Lankapuri maidan) to meet Sri Ram, Sita and Lakshman.

The natural, idyllic, open-air setting of these locations in Akbarpur, uncluttered by props and

Shri Ram Lila Samiti, Aishbagh, Lucknow, (2010).

urban architecture, puts the elaborately costumed performers in stark contrast to the environment. The shine and glitter of the performers' costumes reflected like a thousand jewels in the soft evening light and that of the petroleum lamps.

Below is the Jhanki made of bamboo and covered with a sheet. It is a simple contraption yet very effective. The divinities or swaroopa-s sat this and were carried in procession through the streets, led by beating drums, converting the streets into another performance space.

Wooden Bamboo Frame Jhanki at Akbarpur.

Shatrughana at Akbarpur, (2010).

The Talab or Lake at Akbarpur, (2010).

The saatwik element of devotion is vident here as artiis performed over the Swaroopa-s and darshakas come forward to touch their feetto get their blessings.

The auspicious swastika symbol with a deeya in the middle on a brass Thali. This will be used to perform arti.

Interestingly, at this Lila, although Sita is in exile in the forest, she is never portrayed as an ascetic but always as a queen with her crown and jewellery. The dress of Ram and Lakshman conform to the tradition of ascetics wearing yellow or saffron. Their hairstyle, make-up and jewellery make them

stand out in the darkness of the evening. In different parts of North India, people bring their own traditions and colouring to the performance.

The fourth location of the Akbarpur Ram Lila is in the open-air Ram Lila maidan owned by the organizing Committee and shared by a school and called Lankapuri because of the huge concrete Ravan structure that stands on the Ground. The school uses this Ground as a playground for the rest of the year.

Lankapuri in the open-air Ram Lila maidan, (2010).

Above is the concrete structure of Ravan that remains standing permanently in Lankapuri. Every year, the organizers will build their Ravan putla or effigy and place it in front of this concrete Ravan structure where it will be set alight on the last day of Dussehra. Part of the effigy being built is seen behind the concrete Ravan. The navel of the concrete Ravan is prominent. According to the sacred narrative of the Vaishnava-Hindus, this is where the power of Ravan's immortality resides, and of which he boasts. The beards and faces painted at the top of the effigy symbolize his several heads. There is a seat, suggestive of a throne, carved into the front of this concrete Ravan. .

Musicians sing as they prepare for the arrival of Bharat at Chitrakoot, (2010).

The vyas and musicians set the saatwik tone with sacred songs and chants as they were waited for the arrival of Bharat and Shatrughana in Chitrakoot late at night. The performers use microphones in the open air Chitrakoot setting with a petromax gas lamp by which to read since the electricity supply was interrupted that evening. Coming out late at night for activities like this seems to be the norm as it was around 11 pm and villagers were still gathering for the Lila.

Children come out for Ram Lila.

Percussion Drummers at Akbarpur.

There was a witty exchange in poetry between these performers that brought laughter from the audience.

In Akbarpur, (photo above) percussion drummers lead the swaroopa-s in procession from the starting point of the Sarveshwara Mahadeva Mandir along the streets to the performance area near the Talab. The drums also signal the arrival of the jhanki in the neighborhood.

In photos below, women and girls sit on rooftops to see the Jhanki pass by in the street below.

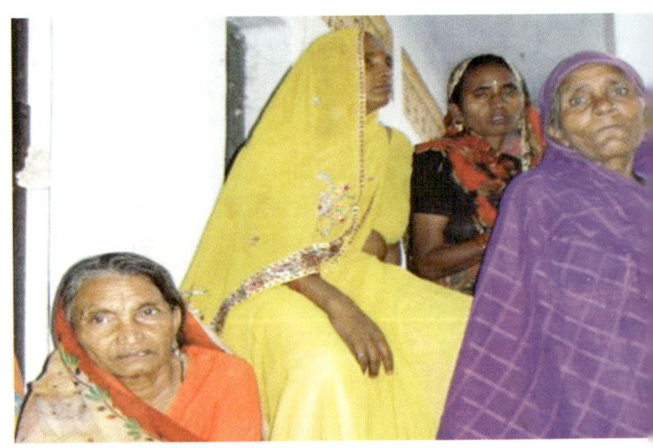

Anvarat Ram Lila at Tulsi Smarak Bhavan, Ayodhya Research Institute (ARI), Ayodhya

Director of ARI, Dr. Y.P. Singh explained that the Tulsi Smarak Bhavan, headquarters of ARI, is affiliated to the Uttar Pradesh (UP) Department of Culture and was founded on August 18, 1986 to research Ram Katha and related issues. Ram Lila takes place here on a daily basis, and not only in the Navratri period. This historic accomplishment is called Anvarat Ram Lila and was started in 2004. It, so far, has only hosted the dramatic/theatrical style of the Lila.

Dr. Yogendra Pratap Singh

Since Mandali-s come from various parts of the country, ARI can show case variations in the dramatic/theatrical style from across the country. YP Singh avers that over forty-six styles of Ram Lila have so far been displayed at ARI. Foreign groups have also performed here.

The Tulsi Smarak Bhavan is a historical site because it is here that Tulsidas began writing the Ramcharitmanas in 1574 CE. This spacewas neglected until the public requested its recognition as a Heritage site. On December 7, 1965, then Governor of Uttar Pradesh, Mr. B. L. Joshi, allotted Rs 522300.00 to build the Tulsi Smarak Bhavan. There is also a museum at ARI that collects art and craft related to Ram Katha from around the country and other parts of the world.

The Tulsi Smarak Bhavan has an in-house theatre that can seat some 500 persons on the carpeted floor. At stage right, there is a manch for the vyas and musicians. There is no entry fee to see the Lila and devotees become regular attendees after a while since they see different performers and styles over the year.

Darshaka-s seated (the elderly on chairs) at the Bhavan's in-house theatre, looking at Ram Lila, (2008).

These Ram Lila performances are exclusively dramatic/theatrical presentations based on Indian aesthetics.

Right : *the Avadh Adarsh Ram Lila Mandali of Patthar Mandir, Faizabad, performs at Tulsi Smarak Bhavan.*

At left : *The drop curtainisbeing lifted to reveal another row of curtains and another setting.*
Photos courtesy : ARI

Right : *Performing Arti before the swaroopa-s.*

At left : *The drop curtain is raised to reveal another row of curtains and another setting. (For more, see Mehta 208-213) All Photos courtesy ARI.*

Left : *Ram in His cradle.*

Right : *The Guru teaches Ram and His brothers the art of archery.*

Orissa artwork showing Bhagvan Jagannath in the avatar of Ram.

Dasanan Ravan (Wooden Handicraft work, Varanasi, U.P., India)

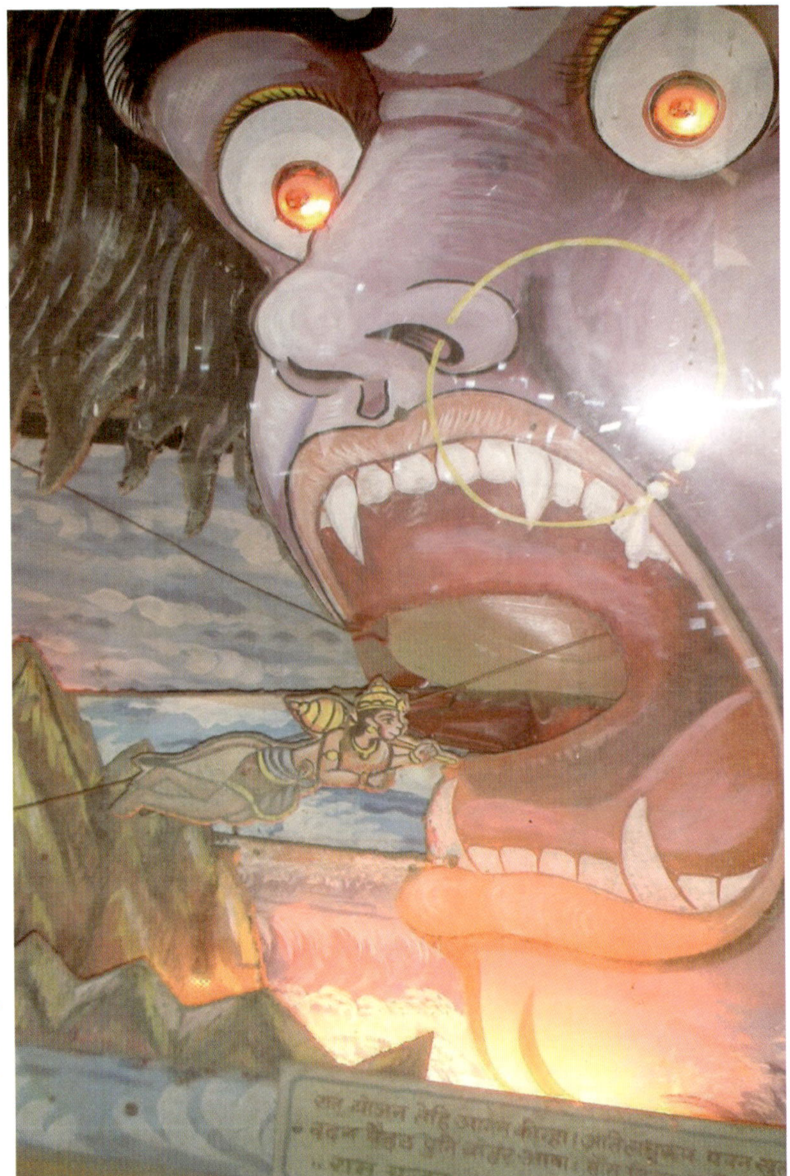

At right, Hanuman flies into the mouth of Surparnakha.

Above : *Dasavtar, Vishnu (Handicraft work Andra Pradesh, India).*

Baal Ram Lila Committee, Japti, Wazirganj, Faizabad

This Ram Lila is some 35 years old, said the organizers. Here the swaroopa-s are called bhagavan. The Lila takes place on a small canopy-covered stage with three sides covered and with two vertical stage curtains that are raised to reveal successive lila-s (events or scenes). While the action is taking place in front of a curtain, the stage area behind is being prepared for the next lila, and the curtain will be drawn to show that event. The downstage area is very narrow (see photo at left). In the photo at left, three male performers dressed as women sing folk songs as a prelude to the Lila.

Their appearance on stage signals that the Lila is about to start. The audience is seated on the ground in front of the stage. This Ram Lila, like others around the city, draws its audience from within the community, and they all are within walking distance.

The Lila starts with dancing and singing by the entertainers. Here one can see the Jester present at the far right. Microphones are used here for dialogue and singing.

Make-up artistes at backstage/green room paint the faces of the young male performers. In the photo above, one can see the Vaishnava sacred marks just painted on the forehead, (2010).

Male dancers dressed as females entertain at the start of the Lila. Folk songs and dancing are a prelude to the Lila, (2010).

Above : *In the Green Room are some of the performers, organizers and children who have come to see the Lila,* (2010).

This Ram Lila takes place on a proscenium stage and therefore bears much similarity with other such styles.

Two performers with an organizer in the Green Room (2010).

Women and children sit on one side to "see" the Lila, (2010).

The saatwik abhinaya dominates as an organizer performs arti over Ram *and* Lakshman *at the start of the Lila,* (2010).

Baxi-ka-TalabDasharaMela (Ram Lila Maidan, Badi Bazaar, Rudhi, Sitapur Road), Lucknow

This Dashara Mela runs for four days with daily performances of both Ram Lila and Krishna Lila.The year 2010 is the first year of the Mela and it should not be confused with the famous Baxi-ka-Talab Ram Lila of Rudhi Village where Hindus and Muslims jointly conduct the Ram Lila, and where Videsh Pal Singh Yadav was the chief organizer (Yadav). Yadav explained that in the year 2010, political boundaries were redefined, making Rudhi Village part of the town of Baxi-ka-Talab. The pradhan is the highest political office in the area and normally becomes the de facto president of the Ram Lila performance. So, the new officials moved the Ram Lila from its traditional spot (next to the famous Baxi-ka-Talab) to the nearby spacious military grounds. There they used professional performers from Mathura/Brindavan for a manch performance that is better known as the Baxi-ka-Talab Dashara Mela.This Mela received heavy funding from Government that threatened the traditional Ram Lila of Baxi-ka-Talab, Rudhi Village. However, the villagers insisted on continuing their Ram Lila. All the houses in the community donated money towards the Ram Lila with no help coming from Government said Yadava, who explained that they needed Rs 3 Lakhs for their three-day Lila.

The Baxi-ka-Talab Dashara Mela, (2010).

The performers were all professionals, and there were huge tents with chairs for audience seating. There were also side screens broadcasting the performance to those who could not directly see the stage performance.

Photo above shows Sita (at Bakshi-ka-Talab, Military Ground) in her silken fineries, elaborate crown, and makeup, (2010).

The side screen at Baxi-ka-Talab Dashara Mela, Ram Lila maidan, Baidi Bazaar, Rudhi, Sitapur Road, Lucknow, (2010).

At Baxi-ka-Talab Dashara Mela (Lucknow) the vyas recites the Ramcharitmanas in traditional style, accompanied here, not by harmonium, but by a modern electronic keyboard. He makes commentaries in the local language. The performers use microphones when delivering dialogue.

In the photo below, at left is the singhasan or consecrated seat of the vyas; in the middle, there is the manch stage with a thrust stage extending out into the audience space.

Krishna Lila is part of this four day Mela. Performances run twice daily - from 2:00 pm there is the Ram Lila and from 8:00 pm, there is the Krishna Lila (2010).

Baxi-ka-Talab, Rudhi Village, Lucknow

The famous Baxi-ka-talab Ram Lila was started in 1972 by founders, Maikoolal Yadav and Muzaffar Husain, said Videsh Pal Singh Yadav, the Pradhan of Rudhi Village and descendant of Maikoolal Yadav. Yadav is the main organizer of this Ram Lila that has won wide publicity for incorporating Muslims in the Ram Lila, a traditionally sacred Hindu performance.

Above photo shows Ravan's court in the open-air space with the Ravan effigy standing behind. The navel region has a circle of electric lights. *Photo courtesy* Baxi-ka-Talab, Rudhi Village Ram Lila Committee

This performance takes place in the open space next to the historically famous talab or pond where there is a permanent Ram Lila covered stage at one end. This space also is known as Bari Bazaar and the Ram Lila Ground. Here, there is no special name for the performers, except Ram who is addressed as *"Bhagavan."* All the artistes come from the village, and they are ordinary farmers and ordinary folks. They become artistes only for the Ram Lila.

During the night of the Lila, there is Nautanki, orchestra, and Jawabi Kirtan, and the performers receive a stipend from the Ram Lila Committee. They also pay for the light and sound, tent and make-up materials associated with the Lila. The Ram Lila performers are not paid any stipend but each artiste receives 100 gm of sweets. The Ram Lila Committee collects money by taking donations from all the houses in their community.

Yadav explained that this year their Lila will run from October 25 to 27 (after this researcher would have left them). First, the committee members go the founder's Samadhi and offer flowers, after which the Lila starts. Last year the Lila ran for four days. On Day One, there were Jhanki-s of Shiva's marriage including a Baraat or wedding procession; on Day Two, there was the birth of Sri Ram and his marriage to Sita; on Day Three there was Sita Haran or kidnapping of Sita and Ravan Vadh or battle with Ravan; and on Day Four, there was Ram Gaddi or installation of Ram as King. In 2010, the Committee planned to perform the following lila-s :

Day One	-	Ram Janam (birth of Ram) and Ram Vivah (marriage of Ram)
Day Two	-	Ram going into exile and up to Bali Vadh
Day Three	-	Ravan Vadh

* *A Baraat is the marriage party of the Dulaha or groom and his guests who journey to the Dulahin's or bride's place for the marriage ceremony.*

In the Ram Lila here, some events are performed on the stage and some in the open air. Day Three is done totally in the open air. Days One and Two are done on the proscenium stage and in the open air.

The performers move in parikrama around the stage when they perform. A Havan at the Durga Ma Mandir (next to the Ram Lila Ground) signals the start of the Ram Lila. They pray also at the nearby Banke Bihari Mandir and Shiva Mandir that are ancient sites.

On the first day, they consecrate the stage and ground with Ganga Jal (holy Ganga water) and the performers do Pranam (obeisance) to earth, after which the Lila starts.

The open-air ground is next to the ancient talab or lake named Baxi-ka-Talab. This will become the performance space for the Ram Lila.

In the photo below there is the permanent, concrete manch that borders the open-air ground where lila-s in the Ram Lila also place.

Here are three performance spaces: the manch, an open raised and temporary manch; and earth as performance space.

Above is the Ravan effigy in the background. Performers mix with the ordinary village boys in the open-air performance space.

The photo above shows folk performers with a variety of instruments and two performers who seem to be dancing with the costume of a donkey in a dance form called 'sumarie'. Left to Right: Masak (bagpipe), Dholak, small Nagara, From Right: Jahnjar, Masak. Foreground and far right: sumarie dancers. The sumarie dance was famous amongst indentured Indians in the Caribbean and rarely seen today.

Organizers and villagers at Rudhi Village, Baxi-ka-Talab Ram Lila, led by Shri Videsh Pal Singh Yadav.
Photos courtesy Baxi-ka-Talab, Rudhi Village Ram Lila Committee.

Bhagwatacharya Smarak Sadan, Sringharhat, Ayodhya

The professional group named Ram Lila Natak Samaj of Orai (Uttar Pradesh) produces this Ram Lila. Here one sees the stage covered on three sides with the audience seated on the ground, facing the stage. There is a middle lane leading up to manch that divides the audience seating area into two – one for women and children and the other for men. A porous wooden barrier separates the seating area. Some people can be seen sitting in this middle lane. Photographers use the middle lane too. Here too, one can see layers of curtains (see below – one green edged curtain and behind it a red edged curtain that allow for one lila (event or scene) to be enacted while the scenery is being set up for a subsequent one.

Above photos shows Ram Lila on the manch at Bhagwadacharya Smarak Sadan, Sringharhat, Ayodhya, (2010).

Above shows Ravan's court at the Ram Lila in Bhagwatacharya Smarak, Sadan, Sringharhat, Ayodhya. Ravan is seated on a simple manch that is his throne while the background is elaborately designed, He uses a microphone. The ornate aharya creates the impression of a rich court (two layers of curtains facilitate changes of scenes)

Jhanki at Bihar Pradeshik Marwari Sammelan: (L to R) Lakshman, Ram and Sita.
Photo courtesy Bihar Pradeshik Marwari Sammelan.

Bihar Pradeshik Marwari Sammelan, Bihar

Arriving in Patna on Oct. 7, 2010, this researcher was met by journalist Mr. Ashish Kumar Mishra of Hindustan Times who had assisted in trying to locate performances in Bihar. Television reports that night warned of Islamic terrorist threats to Navratri festivals and certain popular mandirs in Mumbai.

Mr. Mishra lamented the waning popularity of Ram Lila in recent years. It seems that there is a lack of political and institutional support for Ram Lila. Here, the business community patronizes the Lila, financially.

Mr. Kamal Lopany, Chairman of the Bihar Pradeshik Nawratri Sammelan, informed that they organize the ten-day Ram Lila in that part of the city. They used both a covered manch and the open-air as performance spaces. The swaroopa-s and major performers come from the Radha Saran Mandali of Brindavan. The Sriman Narayan Group comes from Buxar to train the locals for their roles in the Lila. In Patna, the performers use a microphone for their dialogue.

The Ram Lila lasts ten days and runs for three hours daily, in the evening. For the first nine days, it takes place on a manch in the enclosed Thakurbai Hall in Kadamkuan, Patna. On the last day, the Bharat Milap is performed and two Jhanki-s - one with Hanuman and the other with Ram, Sita and Lakshman - (see photo above) – leave Thakurbari Hall and make their way, in procession, through the streets to the Gandhi Maidan. There, the burning of Lanka and the burning of the three effigies of Ravan, Meghnath and Kumbhakaran take place. This falls on Dashami/Dussehra day (Nopany, 2011).

This researcher noted the paucity of Ram Lila performances in and around Patna compared to other cities in Uttar Pradesh, like Lucknow and Ayodhya, and could only see one in the far away town of Buxar in Bihar. There was another in Sitamarhi (north of Bihar) but it was too far away to visit on short notice. This researcher recognizes the tremendous help given by Mr Mishra and Mr Lopany, reflective of the warm hospitality of the people of Bihar.

Buxar, Bihar

Journalists at Hindustan Hindi, Buxar

In Buxar, Bureau Chief and journalists, Pankaj Bharadwaj, Rakesh Kumar Singh, and Ajay Kumar Singh of Hindustan (Hindi daily) served as guides and hosts. According to them, their city's oral history records Ram and Lakshman as having visited Buxar with Guru Vishwamitra. It was here too that Tadka ka Vadha took place at Charitraban in Buxar. The paduka or sandals of Ram are still here in a Mandir named Charanpaduka Mandir, they said.

They explained that the Ram Lila here is 100 years old and runs for 21 days at the Khila Maidan. Things changed over time, they said. In 1980, the Ram Lila moved from the traditional open-air performance of amateur performers to the manch with professional performers. Here the costumes, make-up, jewellery, etc. are all professionally done. The Ram Lila Committee pays for this performance. The performers here are called kalakar or artistes, reflecting their professional status. On the last day of the Lila here, there is Bharat Milan and the Puja Samiti takes out Jhanki-s of Hanuman and different events related to Bharat Milan. The meeting between Ram and Bharat lasts for between one to two hours. The Jhanki-s are taken out around 9 to 10 pm and the procession ends at midnight (Bharadwaj, Singh, and Singh).

Above is the temporary stage covered with a canopy and with several layers of curtains for scene change. The glitter and colour scheme create their own impact in the setting of a bare open-air maidan under artificial lights in the night. Here the audience sits on the floor under covered tents

The Ram Lila is preceded by a short enactment of Krishna Lila. Photos (below) show performers in elaborate costume and makeup

The youthful vyas is the narrator of the Ram Lila. He sits on the singhasan from where he recites the Ramcharitmanas accompanied by an electronic keyboard. Musicians sit at a lower level with their dholaks, harmonium and majeeras, (2010).

King Dasharatha on his throne, (2010).

In Buxar, the performers deliver their dialogue using microphones. Some of them sing for themselves instead of miming. The vachik elements include traditional katha style of recitation (by the vyas), dialogue and singing by the performers.

Above Photo : *Crowds seated in a covered tent with appropriate aesthetic distance between themselves and the stage and separated by a wire fence*, (2010).

Fluorescent tube lights provided lighting in this area.

Goswami Tulsidas Ram Lila Samiti, Sant Tulsipuri, Bhadaini, Varanasi

The Goswami Tulsidas Ram Lila Samiti hosts Ram Lila in one of the narrow streets (gallis) of the neighbourhood of Tulsi Ghat (previously known as Lolarka Ghat and part of Assi Ghat). Here the saatwik abhinaya is dominant. The traditional recitation of the Ramcharitmanas is the centre of focus in the various lila-s or events that are enacted.

Mahant Veer Bhadra Mishra (1939-2013) of Tulsi Ghat was the patron of the Ram Lila at Tulsi Ghat. This researcher discussed with him and in reference to the Ramnagar Ram Lila, the ethical and moral implications of receiving public funding for the Lila, then denying the public permission to videotape what is not a private function and which takes place in public space. He was against denying researchers access to public performances.

The Mahant also reminded this researcher that the Lila at Tulsi Ghat was held in the mohalla (neighbourhood) and attracts devotees of the area. It is not as large scale and ornate as the one at Ramnagar but, he said, "it is what it is." He was right. This Lila has its own charm and is rooted in the landscape and heart of the neighbourhood.

Next to the Mahant's home that is on Tulsi Ghat, there are several small mandir-s. It is here that the young boys gather to get into costume, after school. From here, they quickly make their way through a maze of galli-s (narrow streets) to reach the performance area. The Lila that this researcher saw at Tulsi Ghat was about Kaikeyi demanding her three boons from King Dasharatha, resulting in Sri Ram's exile from Ayodhya. For this, the setting is Kop Bhavan located in a small mandir, under construction, on a bordering elevated site (not seen in the foreground of the photo below). The Ramayani-s sing from the Ramcharitmanas sitting in a circle on the concrete courtyard of a small mandir next to Lolarka Kund. Wooden benches serve as palaces and the performers use spaces in front of the mandir, near the Lolarka Kund and in the mandir under construction.

In the background is the famous Lolarka Kund (behind the fence) and in front of it is a bench that represents Lanka. To the extreme right front is the bench representing Ayodhya that is in front of the small mandir. The singers sit on a simple cotton sheet in the middle of the performance area to recite the Ramcharitmanas. The audience sits next to the singers and on a bench in upper right. It is early in the evening and many more children and adults will join as they return from work and school.

In the photo above the Ramayanis can be seen with the Ramcharitmanas in the middle and musical instruments like harmonium, dholak and majeera. The vyas/pandit reads with use of a portable lamp.

Adult organizers could be seen making their way to the performance area at different times, as some come from work and others, directly from their nearby homes. Children from the neighbourhood filter in and after a while, there are many small children eagerly awaiting the action. It is all very informal though all are disciplined as they enter the performance area. The atmosphere is one of simplicity and familiarity.There is harmony between the event and the environment. The simple scenery is transformed by the costumes of the performers.

Today's Lila–Kaikeyi's Boons–takes place in Kop Bhavan in the mandir under construction (shown in photo below). The vyas recites the lines to the performers, using a torchlight to see, because it is dark and there is is no electricity. Dasharath and Kaikeyi repeat after him in declamatory style, giving that special oratorical effect. The pace of the speech is slower than ordinary daily speech. It is measured and spoken slowly in a kind of sing-song style. This is similar to the style heard at Ramnagar. Here, the performers did not use microphones perhaps because there was no electricity that evening.

L to R : *King Dasharatha, Kaikeyi and the Vyas with torchlight and script*, (2010).

L to R : *Lakshman, Ram and Sita in front of the small mandir. The ornate crowns, costume and make-up transform ordinary boys into swaroopa-s worthy of worship*, (2010).

Third from Left: *Sita, Ram, and Lakshman are seated with the queens and court personnel at their side*, (2010).

Masks at Tulsi Ghat

Below: Mukut Puja- On the first day of the Lila, the purohit consecrates the crowns, bows and arrows, musical instruments etc. through puja.

Right : *Masks used at the Lila*

Photos courtesy
Vahini Geeta Ramsingh

Masks at Ram Lila in Tulsi Ghat

Jaswantnagar, Etawah

The researcher visited Jaswantnagar which is deep inside Bundelkhand, though still in the district of Etawah. The organizers of the Ram Lila proudly informed this researcher that they had met people from the West Indies who came looking for their roots, so they knew about my roots as an indentured Indian.

Journalists Devbrat Gupta, Brijesh Saxena and Sunil Yadav of Dainik Hindustan (Hindi) gave tremendous support in assisting this researcher to get data.

L to R : Dharmendra and Devbrat Gupta, (2010).

> Ravan is not burnt at this Ram Lila. I was told by the organizers that in earlier times there were some people from South India who were involved in the Lila and they objected to the burning of Ravan. ...They make tabeej-s with these pieces of the effigy and they believe them to have magical healing and protective power.

Here, masks are a defining characteristic of the Lila as are the elaborate costumes of their special performers. The two vyas' wear traditional costume of dhoti and kurta, looking like pandits. The performers here use a special kind of yellow make-up on their body.

The divine characters are called swaroopa-s and the terms patra and kalakar refer to the other performers.The swaroopas are all Brahmin boys because they are revered as murtis, said organizers. People touch their feet, the organizers explained. Ravan, they say, can be of any caste, but at death, he is a Brahmin. Only males perform in this Lila. The swaroopa-s here are treated as divinities as daily they get a body massage, have their clothes washed, and Brahmin males cook hot meals for them when the Lila is finished late at night. For ten to thirteen days, the swaroopa-s live at the home of the vyas where they are trained for their roles. They are around fifteen years old. Ram performs his role for two to three years until he is seventeen or eighteen years old.

This Ram Lila runs for fifteen days, followed by a Ras Lila performance for six days, making it a total of twenty-one days of performance. The organizers explain that they perform Ras Lila after Ram Lila because the Krishna avatar came after the Ram avatar. A Ganesh procession also takes place in this Lila. The Lila begins with Ganesh Puja and daily the Ground is purified with Ganga Jal. After performing Ganesh Puja, the organizers, led by kirtan singing, visit homes, stopping for five minutes to perform kirtan. Here, Muslims are the chief artisans for sewing clothing and making Ravan.

The incorporation of the Krishna avatar in Ram Lila is interesting because in places like Ayodhya and Bihar, Devi Worship of Navratri has been growing in recent years and presenting a serious challenge to the traditional Lila-s (Singh).

In Jaswantnagar, the Ram Lila performance lasts between four to five hours daily except on the last day of Dussehra when it runs for between ten to twelve hours. Before the advent of electricity, the Lila was shorter. Nowadays, it is longer. The organizers say they spend approximately ten lakhs (1 lakh = 100,000) of rupees for the twenty-one day performance that includes Ram Lila and Ras Lila.

Ravan is not burnt at this Ram Lila. I was told by the organizers that in the early days there were some people from South India who were involved in the Lila and they objected to the burning of Ravan. The organizers explained that there is a black permanent forty to fifty feet tall concrete statue of Ravan. For Ram Lila, the Ravan effigy is made of bamboo, wood, paper and clothing and this is placed on top of the concrete statue. When Ram shoots the effigy, it falls, signifying Ravan's death. Then people rush to collect parts of the structure and clothing that they take to their homes. They make tabeej-s with these pieces of the effigy and they believe them to have magical healing and protective power. They use if for illness and nazar lag jati hai (bad luck gained from the bad eye or inauspicious glance of someone with bad intentions, jealous mind, and so on).

In photo below, the jhanda is planted in the centre of the Ground, reminiscent of the jarjara pole that was used in ancient Indian theatre.

The equivalent of the Jarjara Pole planted on the Ram Lila Ground at Jaswantnagar, (2010).

The open-air Ram Lila was located in the middle of the town square with its permanent Ram Lila building that housed an office and space for props, costumes etc.

Vedbrat Gupta and relatives who are patrons of the Jaswantnagar Ram Lila, (2010).

A thick steel wire separated the performance space in the open-air Ground from the audience. Women and children stand on one side and men stand on the opposite side. At the southern end, a make-shift covered manch became Lanka. At the northern end, there is a small proscenium stage representing Ayodhya in the Ram Lila building owned by the Ram Lila Committee. The shape of the ground is oblong and resembles a narrow galli or street in India. The performance space is consecrated by organizers and the vyas' who walk around, chanting mantras and sprinkling Ganga Jal or sacred water from the River Ganga.

L to R : Ram, Sita and Lakshman, (2010).

The Photo above shows the divinities at Jaswantnagar. The crowns are large and ornate and the costumes very detailed. Complete with mala-s around the necks of the divinities, the aharya reinforces the view that the performers are murti-s or objects of worship.

At right, *Sita at Jaswantnagar Ram Lila*, (2010).

Lakshman at Jaswantnagar Ram Lila, (2010).

Photo below shows one section of the brass band that circumambulates the Ram LilaGround providing rhythm and beat for the performance. In earlier times, the organizers used nagara drums for the Ram Lila. Police officers are very visible in these performances.

Above : Ravan does a hopping dance as he moves around the performance area pushing and pulling the golden deer with his right hand, while holding his left hand held behind his back. He wears soft shoes while Ram is bare-footed, (2010).

Below is Shabari at Jaswantnagar, (2010).

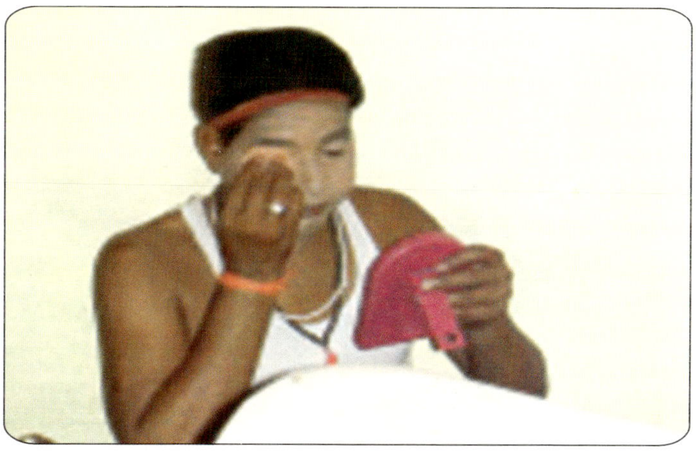

In photo above, a performer puts on his make-up, (2010).

In photo above, Ravan uses a microphone to deliver his lines at the prompt of the vyas who holds the text in his hand, (2010).

Organizers of the Ram Lila (left and above), (2010).

Above: Singers and musicians sit on the ground for this part of the Lila, at Jaswantnagar, (2010).

Masks at Jaswantnagar

Masks have been present in Indian culture as far back as the Mohenjodaro civilization when well-designed baked clay masks, seemingly moulded, with and without horns were found. They wre possibly used as votive offerings and decorations, though they were not large enough for performers to use. In ancient India, dancers impersonating animals or deified animals wore masks (Varadpande 1991:7-15).

In all the Ram Lila performances that this researcher saw in North India, each had a unique charm. Jaswantnagar stands out for its masks and weapons. The Ravan mask, made of metal, is said to be 140 years old. Most of the other masks are made of papier mache. These masks are used by performers primarily in the open-air lila-s. When events take place on the proscenium stage, then make-up and costuming are more elaborate.

Below : *An organizer leads Ravan and Sita toward the Pushpak Viman,* (2010).

Below L to R : *Suparnakha, Ravan and Sita on Pushpak Viman, (2010).*

Suparnakha is elegantly dressed in colourful costume in the photo below right. She draws shrieks of laughter and screams of fear as, with stick in hand, she playfully hits those within reach, (2010).

Left : Ravan in full dress as a sannyasi as he prepares to deceive Sita into crossing the protective Lakshman Rekha, He wears special soft shoes for the Lila. The divinities go barefooted. Organizers and members of the musical band enter the performance area with shoes, (2010).

The kidnapping of Sita is not a dramatic scene of force, power, protest and resistance. Ravan-s actions are tightly controlled, slow and calculated, making it highly dramatic. He jests with the audience in mock attacks on them. His movements are grand and expansive and he is the highlight of this lila. Sita, on the other hand, is passive and moves, almost as in a trance, during the kidnapping action.

The room above (at Jaswantnagar Ram Lila) has a sign that says, "Long Live Lankeshwar (Ravan)." Masks, costumes, and props of Ravan's army are kept here, (2010).

One-Hundred-and-forty-year-old brass mask of Ravan, (2010).

Ravan, in his larger than life mask, kidnaps Sita, (2010).

Above : Mask of Suparnakha, (2010).

MORE MASKS

Devi in the form of Kali, (2010).

Kumbhakaran, (2010).

Rakshaa-s masks, (2010).

Shaiva mark on the forehead of this mask used by a member of Ravan's army, (2010).

Meghnad, (2010).

Vibhishan, (2010).

Hanuman, (2010).

Hanuman's Gadda, (2010).

WEAPONS USED BY RAVAN SENA/ARMY

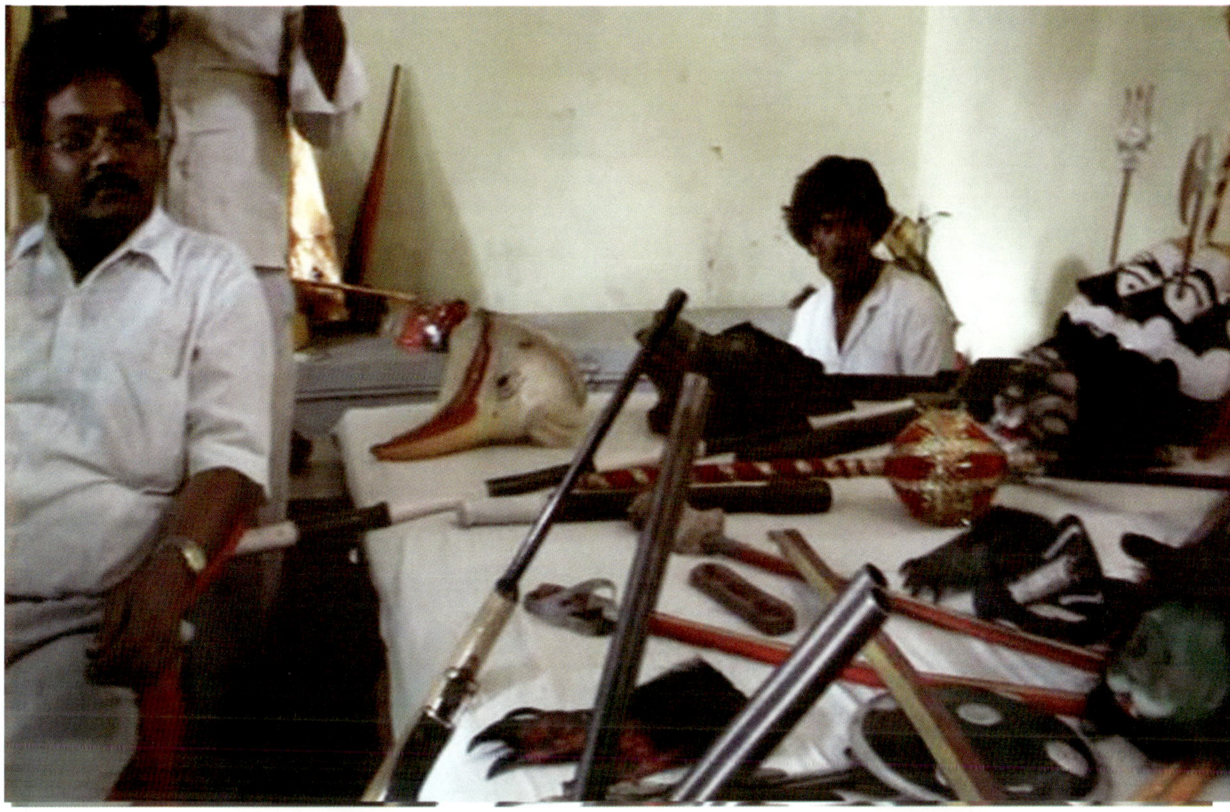

Lanka/Rawan Minar in Kalpi: Where Ravan Does Not Die

The Lanka Minar (Tower) is a 225-foot tall stone tower with the commanding figure of Ravan and family members carved in low relief on its walls. Directly facing the minar is a small Shiva mandir named Chitragupt Mandir and it is in the direct line of vision of Ravan's face, reinforcing his devotion to Shiva. Ram Lila has been performed here since before 1885 (when the Minar was built in honor of Ravan) according to journalists and organizers that this researcher met there. Here, folks are proud that they do not enact the death of Ravan during the Lila. Brajendra Kumar Nigam (descendant of Baba Mathura Prashad Nigam who had conceptualized and built the minar) explained that kings are not killed in the Lila. This convention follows those of Sanskrit theatre where a king is not killed on the stage*. This Lanka minar is part of the history of Kalpi, a city in Jalaun District, Uttar Pradesh is believed to be the birthplace of Ved Vyas who compiled the Mahabharata. The Lila had not yet started when this researcher visited. Here journalists Anil Sharma, KP Singh, and Sunil Sharma from Amar Ujala newspaper, Dainik Jagran and Jana Satta Express, and Raj Narain Shukla of Dainik Aaj provided invaluable assistance in identifying unknown places along the way.

Left : *Brajendra Kumar Nigam and journalists, (2010).*

According to the oral tradition in Kalpi, the architect of the minar (Baba Mathura Prashad Nigam) performed the role of Ravan for so many years that he came to identify with it and he was called Lankesh (another name for

* *According to Mehta (161), there are some plays that do depict death, but "it is generally understood that the representation of death was forbidden in the ancient Indian theatre . . . ."*

Ravan). He built the minar in 1885 in honour of the role that he performed as Ravan. The minar has one hundred and seventy five small steps that lead to the top. Seventy-five-old Brajendra Kumar Nigam is a a descendant of Babu Nigam and an oral historian with a wealth of information.

The Lila usually is held before Navratri or after Divali. In 2010, it was scheduled to be held after Divali. According to Brajendra Kumar Nigam, women used to perform in this Lila long ago, but now only males perform.

Above is the concrete structure where the Dhanush Yajna takes place. This structure is located in the open space in front of the minar where the Ram Lila takes place. The entire Ground looks unkempt and would be cleaned up in readiness for the Lila after Divali 2010.

Lanka or Ravan Minar, (2010).

Journalists also told me about a Ravan mandir that was built by a local king, Maharaja Shiva Shankar, many years back. This mandir is opened once per year on Dussehra day when puja is performed for Ravan's welfare. In Lucknow, there is a group that celebrates Ravan for his intellectual prowess.

Above is part of the courtyard in front of the minar. On the concrete wall is the supine figure of Kumbhakaran. In between the minar and the Shiva Mandir, there is an open courtyard. It is in this space that the Ram Lila takes place.

Purabazar, Faizabad.

In another part of Uttar Pradesh, in Purabazar, Faizabad, the community was more rural than in other Lila performance areas seen by this researcher. The Ram Lila Sangh organizes this Lila which is set in open space with verdant greenery around. It is rustic and natural. Most of the people are dressed in everyday wear. There are many children, but equally present are adult men and women.

Here the costumes and make-up followed the same pattern as elsewhere – where the special characters were more elaborately outfitted, though not by the same standards as of the professional performers elsewhere. The costumes for the special characters resembled those in other parts of North India and seem to be been mass- produced rather than custom-made. Here, the organizers and performers all come from the same community. Children and youths are the main performers in the day's Lila.

Faizabad is a town to which indentured Indians to the Caribbean can trace their ancestors. Indeed, in Trinidad there is a town named Faizabad but it is spelt, Fyzabad. The performance space at Purabazaar is elongated with a bamboo fence demarcating the performance space from audience space.

Arti is performed over Ram and Lakshman in exile. Note their ascetic dress and make-up, (2010).

Through their make-up, dress, hairstyle and decorations, ordinary, young boys are transformed into divinities. In the above photo, the young boys are smeared with ashes to denote their status as ascetics.

Above : Ravan putla that is made with a simple bamboo frame in the shape of a triangle with two long pieces of bamboo for hands. This structure is covered with coloured paper and then set alight on the last day of the Lila, (2010).

Below : a profile of the Ravan putla (effigy)showing its simple construction.

At Purabazaar, the narrator told the story in local dialect, raising and lowering his voice for dramatic effect. Local folk songs and bhajan-s were interspersed throughout the Lila, (2010).

Right : Vanara-s in action, (2010).

Below : Musicians use tabla, harmonium and dholak for musical accompaniment, (2010).

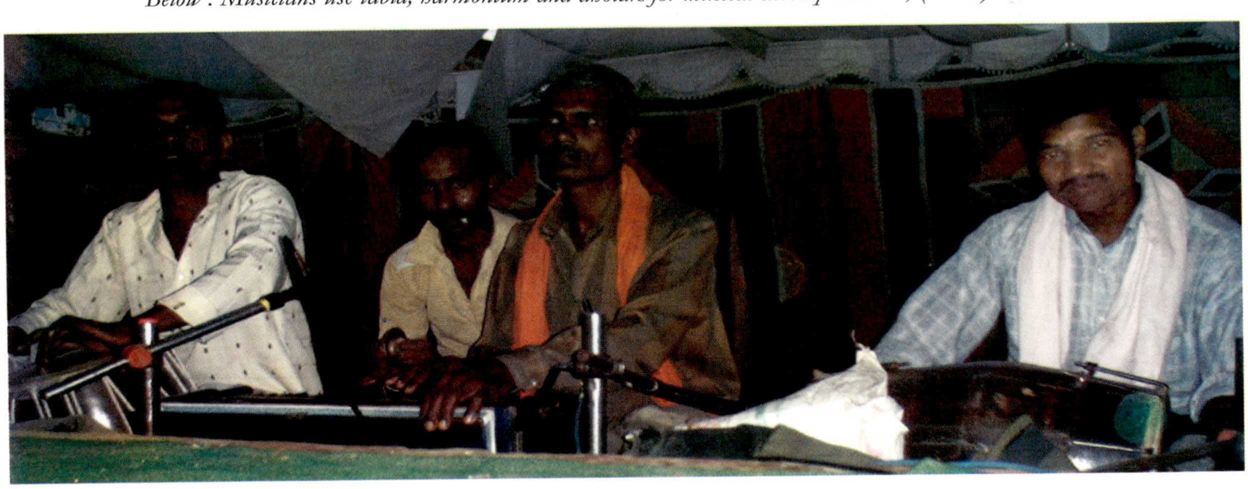

Ravan's throne. Behind is a canvas backdrop with a painted court scene. The prominent fish motif is part of Avadhi art and architecture. It is a popular symbol of good luck and was used in royal insignias, (2010).

Sita dressed like a murti in a mandir, 2010.

Ravan's Court at Purabazaar, Faizabad, (2010).

People stand and move around during the Lila at Purabazaar, Faizabad. The rope barrier (at lower left) separates the audience from performers, (2010).

Above : Organisers of the Lila, (2010).

Rajendra Niwash, Swargdwar, Tulsinagar, Ayodhya

The Ram Lila performance held at Rajendra Niwash, Swargdwar, Tulsinagar in Ayodhya was a professional production by the Mithlanchal Adarsh Ram Lila Mandali coming from Ghulhatta, Bela, Sitamarhi, Bihar. Its director was Pandit Vishnu Prabhakar. This Lila took place in a narrow galli that had been blocked off for this purpose. Like other manch productions by professionals, this one had several curtains that allowed for a quick change of scenery. The audiences sits on the ground.

L to R: Hanuman, Lakshman, Ram and a performer who conducts arti over them, at the start of the Lila, (2010).

A commercially produced Ravan crown, (2010).

Above right : There are several layers of curtains on the proscenium stage, (2010).

Left : *Hanuman's make-up creates the impression of a mask while the monkey in the foreground wears an artificial, plastic mask*, (2010).

Above : *Saatwik rasa is evident as most in the audience raise their hands as a form of praising the Lord in response to the vyas' recitation from the Ramcharitmanas*, (2010).

Above : Performing arti before the singers and musicians, at the start of the Lila, (2010).

Ravan Putla at Tulsinagar, Note the navel region was specially decorated. This putla stood in the narrow galli leading up to the manch where the Lila took place, (2010).

Ramnagar, Varanasi

At right is the entrance to Ramnagar Palace. The Lila takes place in the open field, left and adjacent to the entrance to the palace

There is a temporarily constructed small stage with a covered canopy and a long ramp connecting the small stage to the end stage at the opposite end. This space differs from Jaswantnagar and Purabazaar in that manch-s/stages are used used for the main performance. The Lila moves to different parts of Ramnagar, depending on the plot. Different parts of the town have been permanently named after geographical locations in the Ramcharitmanas.

The devotion and discipline of the audience at this Ram Lila stands out. Here were true darshaka-s with book in hand from which they recited along with the professional Ramayani singers who sang accompanied to jhal-s and harmonium. This is what, in Trinidad, we call Jhal Ramayan and it was the style that the indentured Indians brought with them to the Caribbean. The focus here is the vachik element which emphasizes the singing and hearing of the sacred sound of the Ramcharitmanas. They do not use microphones. The swaroopa-s deliver their dialogue in the oratorical style of a declamation where they speak in slow, measured lines. They listen to the vyas and then repeat the lines. The effect is one where they speak like two words, then pause, then speak another two words and so on. The speech is slow and measured.

Of equal weightage too is the attention given to the saatwik element of "seeing" or darshan of the divine characters. This was dramatized during the arti or waving of lights over the swaroopa-s when quick bursts of artificial light of different colours brightened up the faces of the swaroopa-s drawing exclamations of ecstasy from the darshaka-s. The darshaka-s that come to this Lila come with a very powerful devotional state of mind. They dress in traditional wear, men in dhoti-s and kurta-s and women in their sari-s. They sit on the earthen floor and are segregated, women and children on one side and men on the other.

When this part of the Lila ends, the enactment moved to other parts of the town led by a procession including wooden props like horses, chariots, elephants, etc. This provided spectacle as the procession moved through the streets with people following and others joining along the way. There were many people, however, on the streets selling their vegetables, purchasing, conducting everyday business, etc. and who gave only a cursory glance to the procession.

Soft artificial lights and flares of coloured lights illuminate the faces of the swaroopa-s during arti, 2010.

Above: *Elephants in the Maharaja's entourage with the Maharaja sitting on one as he observes the Lila,* (2010).

In the photo above (left) there is a makeshift tent covered by a galvanize roof on wooden poles complete with chairs, converting it into a wayside stall selling snacks. Two men sell Paan (betel nut). In the photo above (right), two males sell religious books, calendars and other printed materials on the ground, (2010).

In the photo at right, two men are dressed in traditional wear. On their shoulders are the carrying bags with a copy of the Ramcharitmanas and torchlight with the help of which they will read the text as it is being recited by the Ramayan singers, (2010).

The photos below show some of the wooden props on which performers sat as they moved in procession to other parts of the city after the Lila is completed outside the Palace. These wooden props were on wooden wheels and were pulled along the road by men, (2010).

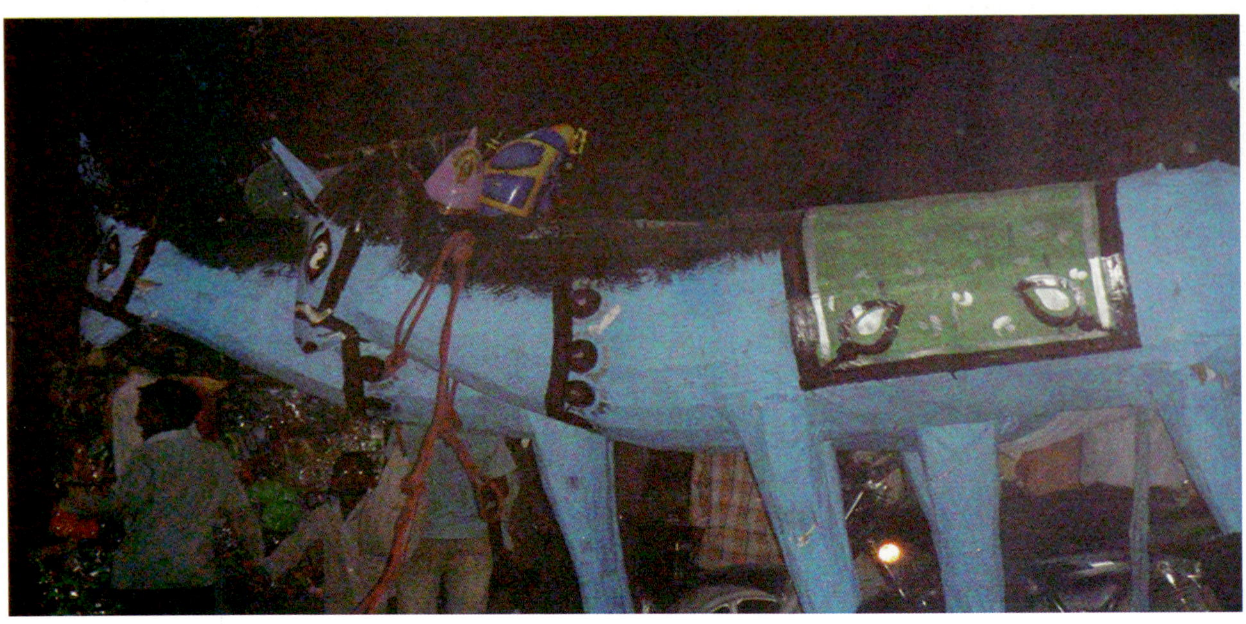

Sahabganj, Ayodhya

At Sahabganj in Ayodhya, a narrow street is blocked off to become the Ram Lila Ground in the city. This Lila, according to the organizers, is one hundred years old and has been performed in the same traditional style over the years. The Ram Lila is organized and produced by the Ram Lila Committee of the Ram Janki Temple Trust. They own and rent out several of their properties and this income is their source of funding for Ram Lila.

Here, the vyas narrated the story in local dialect with the use of a microphone. The performers also used a microphone to deliver their lines. As in many other Ram Lila performances, there was some miming too, for example, when the performers are seated on the wooden horses doing battle, the narration was conducted by the vyas as the performers mimed the action.

At either end of the performance area was a temporarily constructed manch– one for Ayodhya and one for Lanka. Action also took place in the open air space. Chowki-s (wooden tables that serve as beds or for sitting) were placed in the open air performance space for highlighting selected action during the performance.

Left : The chowki or table became the performance space to highlight part of the action. Here, Meghnad performed puja. During the puja, many social and religious norms were mocked. He used a broom for taking water during purification (achman) and hit the priest, whom he called "Pandit," with the broom, drawing laughter from the crowd as the pandit playfully dodged the broom. He next moved to hit the organizers as well. The pandit who is the vyas used a microphone for narration.

One of the highlights of this Lila was the use of wooden horses mounted on a platform with wooden wheels and a long protruding wooden post puller. The two performers, Lakshman and Meghnad, sat and stood on their horses, showing off their skills, during the battle, while others pushed and pulled the horses using the wooden post puller, to facilitate movement of the horses.

Sometimes the performers sat on their own horses as they engaged in battle and at other times both of them were on one horse, much to the delight of the crowds that strained forward to savour the intricacies of battle in this style. Lakshman sat on the horse with his legs under his thighs while Meghnad had his legs hanging down. Hanuman is in the middle (see photo at left).

Right : Lakshman and Meghnad stand on their horses during their fight and they also different kinds of weapons which are handed to them during the fight.

Above : *Meghnad on his horse with bow and arrow in hand*, (2010).

Right : *The wooden platform has a long protruding wooden post puller attached to the front. The horse stands on this. A man manipulates this post puller to move the horse back and forth during the battle*, (2010).

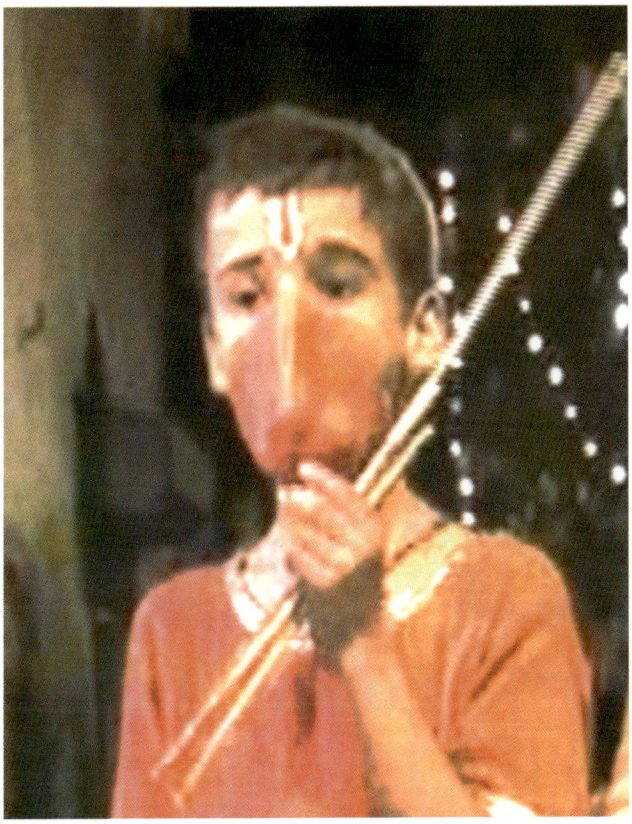

Simple mask over the mouth for young monkey, (2010).

Metal Hanuman Mask, (2010).

Hanuman sits on Meghnad during their battle on the wooden chowki in the open-air, delighting the audience, (2010).

Devi Swaroopa – a young pre-puberty female, (2010).

The cultural landscape in Ayodhya, in particular at Navratri time, reveals a competition between Devi worship and Ram worship. The Navratri chowki-s dominate the physical and cultural landscape. At almost every corner, there is a chowki or devotional program held in small mandir-like temporary structures containing a murti of one of the forms of Devi. The chowki spaces are elaborately decorated with coloured lights, tinsel, etc., and crowds can be seen moving from one chowki to another in a pilgrimage like yatra or journey. Here, people gather to sing bhajans, get darshan of the murti, see the arti being performed, and generally enjoy the mela-like environment where they can buy things, eat out, and socialize late into the night.

The Ram Lila performance, on the other hand, because it took to the proscenium stage in the open maidan, has lost that mela-like environment and freedom of movement that characterizes the older form of Ram Lila in the open air. This older form of Ram Lila still characterizes Ram Lila in Trinidad and Suriname. Today, in most of the Ram Lila-s in North India, the devotees arrive, sit on the ground as disciplined theatre-goers and look up to the manch to "see" the Lila, then they get up and leave quietly. Where the Ram Lila is performed in the open air, e.g. Jaswantnagar and Akbarpur, one notices a more vibrant atmosphere and greater public participation.

Above : At Sahabganj, the sacred marks on the forehead of the above performers indicate that the left performer is a devotee of Shiva while the performer at right is a devotee of Vishnu, (2010).

Organizer with three membes of Ravan's army. Their make-up stands out for its simplicity and effectiveness, (2010).

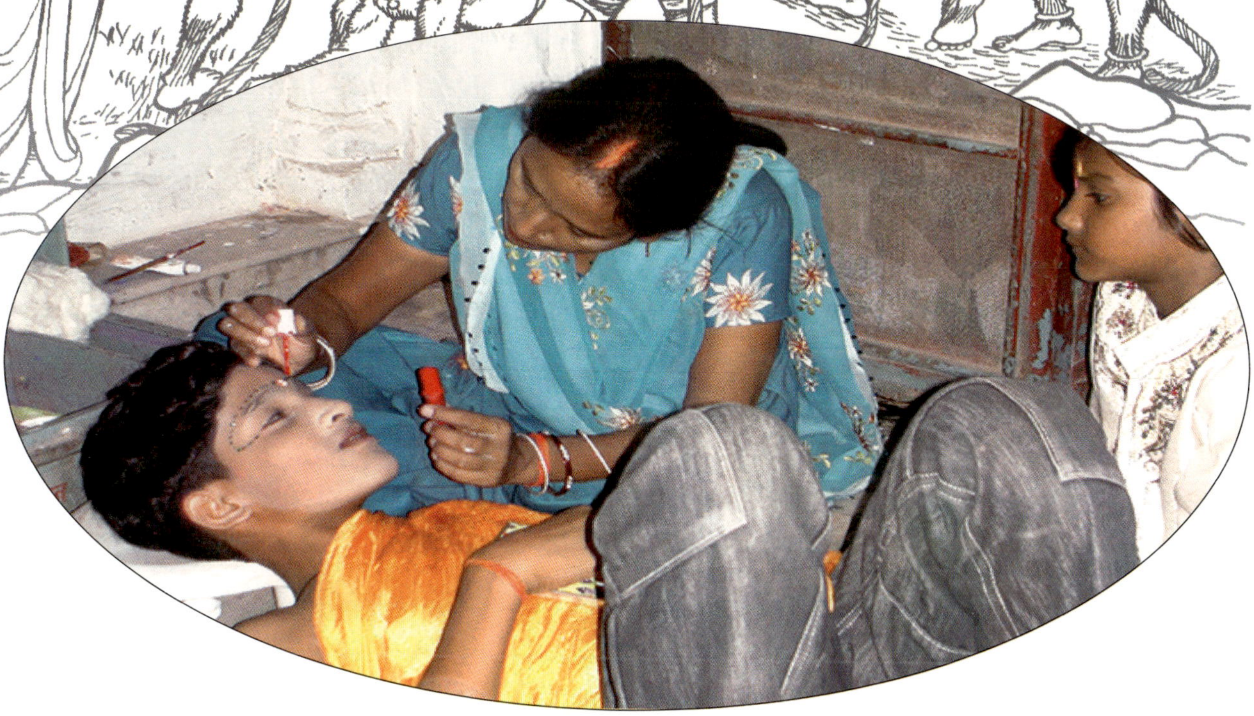

Mother puts on make-up on son, (2010).

Drummers provide the beat and rhythm for the fighting scenes, (2010).

Ravan putla or effigy at Sahabganj, (2010).

Above : An organizer at the Lila, (2010).

Father and Daughter come to "see" the Lila, (2010).

At right, is a putla of Hanuman. This was kept at the Shri RamJanki Mandir, in Sahabganj, Faizabad. This mandir organizes the Ram Lila in Sabahganj, (2010).

Below : Dharmendra, his wife and other family members come out to "see" the Lila late at night, after walking through the town to see the earlier Navratri pandals, (2010).

Sri Ram Lila Samiti, Konch, Jalaun, Bundelkhand

The people of Konch are warm and welcoming as the people in all other Ram Lila-s of North India.. Here, Ram Lila organizers, villagers and young children greeted me with great interest and were very pleased about the research in their Ram Lila traditions.Bottom Left photo shows the researcher (in the middle) meeting with residents and journalists (right) at Konch.

Sri Dharmada Rakshini Sabha, Konch, Jalaun, Registration Number 47/1927-28 founded Sri Ram Lila Samiti of Konch. The Lila was conducted by the late Badri Prasad Seth Sikriwale. According to Ayodhya Prasad Gupt Kumud, it was Chaudhary Biharlal Gaur who started the first Lila in 1851, performing different lila-s (events) in fourteen gardens that bordered Konch. This converted the entire area of Konch into performance space. However, in 1910, this changed when the performance shifted to a platform stage in the maidan.

At Konch, the Lila starts very late at night. On some days, the proscenium stage is used for the Lila. On the evening that this researcher visited the Ram Lila, it took place on a proscenium stage set in the concrete Ram Lila Committee's building. In front of it was open-air space - a long rectangular area that was demarcated within the town square. On other days, especially when the yuddh-s or wars (e.g. Rawan Yuddh, Marich Yuddh) take place, such lila-s (events) took place in open air space.

Here the swaroopa-s were called murti-s . Long ago, these murti-s lived at the home of the vyas but nowadays they live in the Ram Lila building for fifteen days prior to the Ram Lila.

The audience sat on the ground in the open-air looking up at the performance in the proscenium stage. They were also segregated by gender.The declamatory speeches of Lakshman and Hanuman brought loud cheers from the audience.

Above : *The small proscenium stage with musicians seated at stage right and one at stage left. The scenery consists of plants and a painted backdrop. The performers can be seen in the middle of the stage. The audience is seated at the front,* (2010).

Live singers and musicians deliver traditional folk songs, bhajans, and music, (2010).

The performers on stage spoke slowly but a little faster than in Varanasi. Here they spoke a whole sentence like in daily speech, whereas in Ramnagar and Varanasi they spoke approximately two words at a time in declamatory style. Besides dialogue, popular folk song and bhajans were included as part of the storytelling. For example, at Konch, Shabari sang about the glories of Shri Ram. The singing is of professional quality and musicians accompany the singers. There are many microphones on the stage.

During some of the action, like when Hanuman bowed to Ram having recognized him as the avatar, the folk singers heightened the rasa of the moment with rich rustic singing. The tabla player strategically punctuated Hanuman's passionate speech to Ram, with vigorous taps of the table, adding drama to the enactment and rasic appreciation in the audience. Some of the action was mimed. For example, when Hanuman lifted Ram and Lakshman on his shoulders, the narrator told the story while the performers enacted it.

In most Ram Lila-s, a prompter helps the young children with their lines. Here in Konch, the prompter stays out of sight, behind a tree prop, from where he prompts the performers.

The Vyas acts as prompter with text in hand and standing out of sight behind a tree prop, (2010).

Meeting with residents of Konch

Shri Shishu Baal Ram Lila Samiti, Phool Wali Gali*, Lucknow

In Lucknow, the Shri Shishu Baal Ram Lila Samiti conducts their Lila on the proscenium stage in Khulapreksha Griha, Phool Wali Gali, Nepali Park Bag Tola Chowk. The audience sat on the floor looking up at the Lila on the manch, 2010.

The stage has a three-dimensional painted backdrop that, with lighting effects, created the illusion of depth.

A spotlight of one colour focuses on the Ravan (photo at left) while the rest of the stage is another color, (2010).

A rudimentary and effective system provides different coloured spotlighting on the stage, (2010).

* *Phool = flowers; wali = the one with; gali = narrow street. In other words, the street with a lot of flowers; it is indeed the flower market of the area.*

All the divine characters were called swaroopa-s here. The main performers were children but adults did perform some roles, for example, as Ravan. The folk singers and musicians were also adults. The organizers here insisted that this performance is not a natak but pure Lila.

This Ram Lila was very musical with lots of local folk songs interweaved into the plot. The musical group used instruments like harmonium, tabla, etc. Young teenage boys lustily recited the verses of the Ramcharitmanas, demonstrating what they had learned thus far under their guru. As the name, Phool Wali Gali, suggests fresh flowers were in abundance here. Two vyas' narrated at this Lila. One was seated and the other was standing. They both told the story in mixed song and speech style.

Ravan with garlands of fresh flowers around his neck and his wrists, (2010).

Ravan was seated for most of the time. He used his voice, upper body and hands for communicating meaning, (2010).

Left: Hanuman wears a crown. His wrist, arms and neck are decorated with fresh flowers and he carried a gadda or mace, (2010).

Organizers of the Lila, perform arti over Ram, Lakshman and Hanuman. Ram and Lakshman are ascetics in exile as indicated by their clothing, hairstyle, and bow and arrow. The facial make-up and Vaishnava mark on the forehead stand out in the makeup, (2010).

The painted backdrop is a modern scenery showing cars and skyscraper building and not in harmony with the Lila event being enacted.

The singers are accompanied by traditional instruments like dholak, harmonium, tambourine etc.

In photo left, the narrator uses the Ramcharitmanas text from which he chants during his narration, (2010).

In the photo at above, the jester speaks using a stationary microphone, (2010).

Ram and Lakshman on the throne, (2010).

Sri Public BalRam Lila Samiti, Lila Ground, Lohiyaa, Chowk, Lucknow

This researcher was able to catch a short part of the Ram Lila produced by the Sri Public Ram Lila Samiti also called Shri Public Bal Ramlila Samiti. This was near to the Shri Shishu Baal Ram Lila Samiti, Phool Wali Gali in Lucknow.

The make-up and costumes adhered to Indian aesthetics but the painted backdrop suggesting depth resembled the one at the nearby Shri Shishu Baal Ram Lila Samiti in Phool Wali Gali and was out of synch with the story being told. Here, a short skit related to farmer's issues was enacted before the Ram Lila began. There were comic moments in the skit.

Two performers in the skit against the modern backdrop, (2010).

Musicians with traditional instruments, (2010).

Left: *The Jarjara Pole stands outside the Shri Public Bal Ramlila Samiti performance space. A ritual with flowers was performed at the base of the pole, indicated by the strewn flowers and water,* (2010).

Details of the picture of Hanuman at the base of the Jarjara Pole, with the text "Shri Hanumate Namah" – This pole stands out at the Shri Public Bal Ramlila. Only at the Ram Lila in Jaswantnagar did this researher see another jarjara pole, (2010).

Audience space under the temporarily constructed canopy tent, (2010).

Above : The make-shift puja sthaan with photographs that are popularly used in worship. Performers worship here before the performance, (2010).

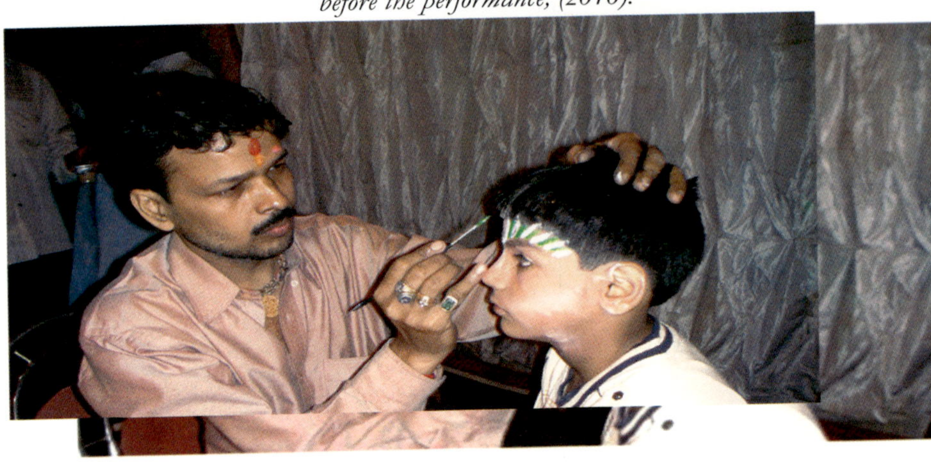

Above : Getting ready, (2010).

Indira Gandhi National Centre for the Arts (IGNCA) and Sangeet Natak Akadami

Between October 20 and November 20, 2010, the IGNCA and Sangeet Natak Akadami (SNA) held a celebration of masks, puppets and picture showmen traditions of India, at IGNCA's headquarters, No. 3, Dr. Rajendra Prasad Road, New Delhi. On Oct. 26, 2010, this researcher saw snippets of the Ram Lila artform from different parts of India,

Ram stylistically prepares to shoot the enemy, (2010).

Rakshasa with sword in hand, (2010).

The percussionists provide appropriate beat and rhythm as Ram stylistically walks, (2010).

Sita and her saheli (friend) walk stylistically to the beat of the percussionists, (2010).

Ram Lila in Mauritius

This researcher was surprised to learn that Mauritius did not have a vibrant ten-day open-air Ram Lila tradition. After all, they had the largest number of girmitiyas (Mishra 233) and they were renowned in the diaspora for having retained strong Indian cultural traditions and for still speaking Indian ancestral languages in their homes, while other parts of the diaspora had either lost or were losing theirs.

Hanuman in an excerpt from Ramcharitmanas by Navyuga Arts Group, (2010).

Raghoonath Deeal, (2010).

They brought with them their Ramayana and their traditions and the Kunwar Vijaymal (an epicrevered by Kali devotees), said Ragoonath Deeal*. Hazareesingh, writing about cultural life between indentureship and 1950, noted the presence of regular, weekly religious events. So entrenched was the Ramcharitmanas (Ramayan) that Mauritius came to be known as Ramayan country, with local legends about its creation being linked to the Ramayan.

Mauritius has many self-sustaining Ramayan Mandali-s that hold weekly satsangh-s. During Chaitra Navratri (start of the Hindu year in March-April) and at Divali time, these mandali-s have jhanki-s of the Ramayan. In addition to performances of Ramayan, the popular folk performances included the Vishnu Avatar, Krishna Lila, etc. The Navyuga Arts Group in Mauritius has presented hundreds of plays in English, Kreol, Bhojpuri and Hindi. This group presents half hour performances based on Ramayana for Divali. The most popular dramatization is the Ram-Ravan Yuddh (battle) which they have been staging for the last twenty-five years (Deeal).

Deeal who was born in 1948 said that his uncle, twenty years his senior, was an artiste with a performing group that went from village to village to perform. This was the popular form of entertainment at the time, since there were no cinemas then. Then came the silent cinema in the 1930s followed by the sound cinema in the 1940s and this negatively affected the folk performances in rural communities. People were drawn to the new cinema medium sending the folk performances into decline.

However, the rural folk performers then took their performances to the apron stage in the cinema. Deeal recalled a Ram Lila performance being held in the Fond-du-Sec region in a cinema hall. He recalled, too, the time when the flying Hanuman fell after someone cut the rope at the wrong time.

Writer, Abhimanyu Unnuth gifts a copy of his book, Slices from a Life, to this researcher, (2010).

* Deeal is a Ramayani since childhood and comes from a Shivnaraini and Ramayani family. He teaches Ramayan and Hinduism across Mauritius and previously served as a teacher, journalist, chief editor at Mauritius Broadcasting Corporation, and Hindu member of the Council of Religions.He is Sanghchalak of Hindu Swayamsewak Sangh (Mauritius) and Trustee of the Board of Trustees, Central Vishwa Hindu Parishad. He also conducts purohit training classes and regular Ramayan Katha-s and

Performances like Ram Lila, Inder Sabha, Dasavtar, and Krishna Lila moved to the cinema hall between 1940 and 1960 when excerpts of the Ramcharitmanas were enacted for one to two hours on the stage. A major factor that pushed the performances from the open-air to the cinema hall was that of the rains (Deeal, 2011). Two major events in that period would have been World War II (1939 to 1945) and the struggle leading up to political Independence that came in 1968.

The folk mandali-s and folk performances were once popular in Mauritius but went into decline in this period. The following factors contributed to this decline (Deeal):

1. There was change in entertainment tastes in successive generations as they moved away from the traditional forms of rural entertainment to the new forms of mass communication like the cinema.
2. There was little or no financial patronage from the community to sustain mandali-s whose artistes were all volunteers.
3. Males started shying away from performing female roles. Deeal recalled that his older cousin, Rambirich, performed the female role in either the Inder Sabha or Ram Lila (he did not clearly recall which one). It took over one hour to remove the make-up and he was taunted by fellow artistes and friends for performing a female role. Women were not allowed to perform in the public in those days.
4. Pride in the folk language of Bhojpuri declined as the new Hindi movies invaded Mauritius. The Indians moved away Bhojpuri, its culture like Ram Lila and the other performing arts, to the Hindi of the new movies.
5. Sudden and excessive rains also negatively affected the outdoor performances.

Despite these stresses on the Indian folk culture, Deeal said that excerpts from the Ramayan and performances like the Narsimha Avatar and Krishna Lila continued to be practised over the years. Women started performing in public and some even headed mandali-s which were either dominated by or exclusively female. However, they co-opted men to work with them in male character roles.

The Navyuga Arts Group in Mauritius has performed many dramatic performances in English, Kreol, Bhojpuri and Hindi and for the last twenty-five years, they have been performing half-hour dramatizations of Ramayan at Divali time, with the Ram-Ravan Yuddh being the most popular of them. The advent of local programming in the newly introduced television medium in 1965 and the new Ministry of Arts and Culture following Independence in 1968 were catalysts in the local arts, which focused on contemporary issues rather than the ethnic Indian folk arts. The staging of Ram Lila excerpts went into decline (Ragoonath).

Today, as evidenced by the work of Navyuga Arts Group, ethnic Indian folk performances remain alive in Mauritius, though not as rich and varied as before.

Dr. SarIta Boodoo oversees the annual Havan at Apravasi Ghat to mark the arrival of Indians in Mauritius. She launched her new book, "Speak Bhojpuri" at this function.

Writing in 1950, Hazareesingh (127-128) noted that theatrical performances were performed occasionally in Indian villages with Ram Lila and Indra Sabha being the more prominent ones. He recalled that in 1920, artistes had come from India to revive the Indian arts in Mauritius and their presentations were of a high standard. He noted that the local Indians would take up the theatrical arts some twenty years later. Ram Lila had certainly gone into decline and many lamented the loss of the folk performing arts. These included Ragoonath Deeal, Dr. Sarita Boodoo, Suresh Ramburn, Veenaud Boodhun, Jugdishwur Goburdhun, and Abhimanyu Unnuth.

Eighty year old, Sir Anerood Jugnaut (1930-) President of Mauritius, said that although his elders spoke about having seen Ram Lila, he never saw it himself. He shared this cultural loss with forty-six year old President Bharrat Jagdeo (1964 -) of Guyana, who also had heard about Ram Lila from his father but never saw one until he came to Trinidad in 2009, at this researcher's invitation.

In the early 1970s, at the football ground in Triolet, there was a one-day performance of Ramcharitmanas that was called Ram Lila (Unnuth). Indian diplomats helped to design the festival, which started around 7:30 pm and ended at 10 or 11 pm. It included a cultural program. Three effigies of Ravan (20-25 feet tall), Kumbhakaran (15 feet tall), and Meghnath (15 feet tall) were set alight in the open ground. Ram and Lakshman came in their chariot and Ram arrows that were set alight. Mahesh Ramjeeawun was the stage manager for that performance (Deeal). It seems that the Member of Parliament for the region had to deal with objections from the Tamil community over the burning of Ravan and so he decided to exclude this event from Ram Lila in Troilet, thereafter.

L to R: VeenaudBoodhun author, and VidyaBoodhun at President's House in Mauritius, (2010).

Dr. Sarita Boodoo, scholar and cultural activist, said that Ram Lila used to be staged as street plays along with Krishna Lila in the villages in the baithkar-s and village squares. She recalled conducting a Seva Shivir with others in the village of Belle Vue Maurel in the 1970s, when they produced one week of Divali celebrations along with a one-day Ram Lila. Then, in 1983, in Quatre Bornes, she was again involved in producing a one-day Ram Lila performance for Divali as a national festival (Boodoo). Suresh Ramburn, a research assistant and cultural activist explained, as did writer Abhimanyu Unnuth, that there were some tensions between ethnic Tamil Hindus and other Hindus over the burning of Ravan in earlier times and especially when it happened in Triolet in the early 1970s. It was in deference to this sensibility that huge performances of Ram Lila were stopped in earlier

Apravasi Ghat in Mauritius – the first port of entry for the indentured Indians coming to Mauritius. They entered via these steps, (2010).

Above : *Jugdishwur Goburdhun, current Mauritius High Commissioner to India, and President, Kissan House, Coudan, one of my hosts in Mauritius,* (2010).

years and certainly after the 1970s (Ramburn).

Following the political decision to stop burning of the Ravan effigy at Triolet, Mauritius experimented with producing the open air Ram Lila without the burning of the Ravan effigy. By excluding the burning of the Ravan effigy, the audience missed the opportunity to experience the resolution or denouement of the story. They would have left unsatisfied having not experienced the end of the story. The last day of an open-air day Ram Lila is important for that collective and individual experience. It is usually the day that draws the largest crowds. Perhaps the exclusion of the burning of Ravan led to the death of the open-air Ram Lila in Mauritius. The issue of burning Ravan was addressed both at Jaswantnagar and Kalpi in India and treated in a different way, with the Lila remaining vibrant.

In conclusion, Ram Lila as a traditional ten-day folk festival performed within ritual time (i.e. starts with Sharad Nawratri and ends on Dussehra day), either on the manch or earth as the stage is not present in Mauritius today. Some say they heard of the open-air LILA style and how it then moved to the stage. Today, Ramayan groups still have short enactments of Ramcharitmanas on stage.

The effect of a community coming together to plan and produce their own Ram Lila is a very empowering tool in community life. As recognized by UNESCO, this performance captures the cultural diversity of a people and is essential to their identity. It is hoped that Ram Lila will attain equal status with another of UNESCO's projects in Mauritius, viz. the Apravasi Ghat project, which, on July 12, 2006, was inscribed on the World Heritage List at the 30th session of UNESCO'S World Heritage Committee held in Lithuania ("Aapravasi Ghat").

Meeting with the Hon. Mookeshwar Choonee, Minister of Arts & Culture in, (2010).

Select Bibliography

Aapravasi Ghat. UNESCO, whc.unesco.org/en/list/1227.

Akhyan, A Celebration of Masks, Puppets and Picture Showmen Traditions of India. Akhyan, A Celebration of Masks, Puppets and Picture Showmen Traditions of India, www.ignca.nic.in/PDF_data/aakhyan_brochure.pdf.

Awasthi, Suresh, and Richard Schechner. "'Theatre of Roots': Encounter with Tradition." Tdr (1988-), vol. 33, no. 4, 1989, pp. 48–69., doi:10.2307/1145965.

Balkaransingh, Satnarine. The Shaping of a Culture. Hansib, 2016.

Behan, T. L. Bulletins and Other State Intelligence for the Year 1858. Harrison and Sons, 1860.

"Bharat Milap at Nati Imli Finds Rapt Attention." Timesofindia, The Times of India, 18 Oct. 2010.

Bonnemaison, Sarah, and Christine Macy. "The RamLila in Ramnagar." Design Quarterly, no. 147, 1990, pp. 22–23., doi:10.2307/4091217.

"The Curtain." Sanskrit Play Production in Ancient India, by Tarla Mehta, Revised ed., V, Motilal Banarsidass Publishers, 1999, pp. 208–213. Performing Arts.

Das, Sisir Kumar. A History of Indian Literature: 1800-1910 Western Impact: Indian Response. Sahitya Akademi, 1993.

Gooptar, Primnath, and Pundit Bhownath Maraj. The Ramleela of Sangre Grande: from a Rural Town in Northeast Trinidad: Celebrating 25 Years of the Sangre Grande Ramleela Committee 1990-2015. Sangre Grande Ramleela Committee, 2015.

Hazareesingh, K. A. A History of Indians in Mauritius. General Print & Stationery, 1950.

Hein, Norvin. The Miracle Plays of Mathura. Yale University Press, 1972.

Iravati. Performing Artistes in Ancient India. D.K. Printworld, 2003.

Jain, Isha. "Flying Hanuman a Major Draw at Aishbagh Ram Lila." The Times of India, 16 Oct. 2010.

Kapur, Anuradha. Actors, Pilgrims, Kings, and Gods: the Ramlila at Ramnagar. Seagull Books, 1990.

Khandelwal, Brij. "Krishna Lila Comes Alive on Streets of Agra." Punjab Newsline , 15 Nov. 2010.

Kumud, Ayodhya Prasad Gupt. Sanskritik Bundelkhand. Naman Prakashan, 2004.

Lidova, Natalia. Drama and Ritual of Early Hinduism. IV, Motilal Banarsidass Publishers, 1996.

Lutgendorf, Philip, et al. "Indian Theatre and the Inside-Outsider." Tdr (1988-), vol. 36, no. 4, 1992, p. 162., doi:10.2307/1146224.

---. The Life of a Text: Performing the Ramcaritmanas of Tulsidas. University of California Press, 1991.

Mehta, Tarla. Sanskrit Play Production in Ancient India. Motilal Banarsidass Publishers, 1999.

Mishra, Amit Kumar. "Indian Indentured Labourers in Mauritius." Studies in History, vol. 25, no. 2, 2010, pp. 229–251., doi:10.1177/025764301002500203.

Rampersad, Indrani. "'Ram Lila in Trinidad, Suriname and Guyana." Encyclopaedia of Hinduism, vol. 6, India Heritage Research Foundation and Rupa & Co., 2011.

---. "The Ram Lila/Ramdilla Jhandi." Nidan, 21 Dec. 2011, pp. 110–126.

---. "Hinduism in the Caribbean." Contemporary Hinduism, edited by P. Pratap Kumar, Acumen Publishing, 2013, pp. 57–66.Kumar, P. (Ed.). (2013).

---. "Ram Lila." Encyclopedia of Indian Religions, Edited by Arvind Sharma et al., Springer, Dordrecht, 2018, doi.org/10.1007/978-94-024-1036-5_420-1.

Richmond, Farley P., et al. Indian Theatre: Traditions of Performance. M. Banarsidass, 2007.

"The Samba of Roda and the Ramlila Proclaimed Masterpieces of the Oral and Intangible Heritage of Humanity." UNESCO, 25 Nov. 2005, portal.unesco.org/en/ev.php-URL_ID=30973&URL_DO=DO_TOPIC&URL_SECTION=201.html.

Sax, William S. "The Ramnagar Ramlila: Text, Performance, Pilgrimage." History of Religions, vol. 30, no. 2, 1990, pp. 129–153., doi:10.1086/463218.

Schechner, Richard, and Linda Hess. "The Ramlila of Ramnagar [India]." The Drama Review: TDR, vol. 21, no. 3, 1977, p. 51., doi:10.2307/1145152.

"Section d, The Curtain." Sanskrit Play Production in Ancient India, by Tarla Mehta, Motilal Banarsidass Publishers, 1999, pp. 208–213.

Singh, Isha Priya. "Lucknow Ki Machhliya'n ." The Lucknow Observer, 5 Nov. 2014, lucknowobserver.com/lucknow-ki-machhliyan/.

Sullivan, Bruce M. "Dying on the Stage in the Natyasastra and Kuttiyam: Perspectives from the Sanskrit Theatre Tradition." Asian Theatre Journal, vol. 24, no. 2, 2007, pp. 422–439., doi:10.1353/atj.2007.0041.

Thiara,, Ravinder K. "Indian Indentured Workers in Mauritius, Natal and Fiji." Contents of The Cambridge Survey of World Migration 95016842, catdir.loc.gov/catdir/toc/becites/genealogy/immigrant/95016842.toc.html.

Varadpande, Manohar Laxman. Concise Dictionary of Indian Theatre. Abhinav, 2007.

---. History of Indian Theatre: Loka Ranga, Panorama of Indian Folk Theatre. Abhinav Publications, 1992.

Vatuk, Ved Prakash, and Sylvia Vatuk. "The Ethnography of 'Sang," A North Indian Folk Opera." Asian Folklore Studies, vol. 26, no. 1, 1967, p. 29., doi:10.2307/1177698.

Vibhuti Narain Singh, Maharaja of Banaras:1927-2000. TDR/The Drama Review, vol. 45,

Interviews

Bihar Pradeshik Marwari Sammelan. Ram Lila in Patna. Personal Interview. Patna.

Bharadwaj, Pankaj, Rakesh Kumar Singh and Ajay Kumar Singh of Hindustan (Hindi daily)."Buxar Ram Lila." Personal Interview. 8 Oct. 2010.

Boodhun, Veenaud. "Ram Lila in Mauritius." Personal Interview. 4 Nov. 2010.

Boodoo, Sarita Dr. "Ram Performance Traditions in Mauritius."Telephone Interview. 4 Nov. 2010.

Deeal, Ragoonath. "Mauritius Ram Lila." Personal Interview. 4 Nov. 2010.

Kumud, Ayodhya Prasad Gupt. "Konch Ram Lila." Personal Interview. 13 Oct. 2010.

Maharaj, Pandit Birju. "Ram Lila in Uttar Pradesh." Personal Interview. 11 Nov. 2011.

Mehta, Bhanu S. "The First Ram Lila." Personal Interview by author. January 10, 2009.

Ramburn, Suresh. "Ram Lila across Mauritius." Personal Interview. 4 Nov. 2010.

Ramsingh, Geeta Vahini. Ram Lila in Benares. Personal Interview. 5 Feb. 2011

Singh, Yogendra Pratap. "Ram Lila in Uttar Pradesh." Personal Interview, 10 Oct. 2010.

Unnuth, Abhimanyu. "Indian Culture in Mauritius." Personal Interview. 4 Nov. 2010.

Yadav, Videsh Pal Singh. "Baxi-ka-Talab Ram Lila". Personal Interview. 18 Oct. 2010.

Emails

Deeal, Ragoonath, Message to the author. 25, 28 April 2010. E-mail.

Nopany, Ekta. 23-25 April 2011. Email